THE COMPLETE IDIOT'S GUIDE® TO

Pizza and Panini

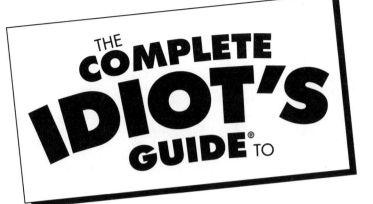

Pizza and Panini

by Erik Sherman

ALPHA

A member of Penguin Group (USA) Inc.

ALPHA BOOKS

Published by the Penguin Group

Penguin Group (USA) Inc., 375 Hudson Street, New York, New York 10014, USA

Penguin Group (Canada), 90 Eglinton Avenue East, Suite 700, Toronto, Ontario M4P 2Y3, Canada (a division of Pearson Penguin Canada Inc.)

Penguin Books Ltd., 80 Strand, London WC2R 0RL, England

Penguin Ireland, 25 St. Stephen's Green, Dublin 2, Ireland (a division of Penguin Books Ltd.)

Penguin Group (Australia), 250 Camberwell Road, Camberwell, Victoria 3124, Australia (a division of Pearson Australia Group Pty. Ltd.)

Penguin Books India Pvt. Ltd., 11 Community Centre, Panchsheel Park, New Delhi—110 017, India

Penguin Group (NZ), 67 Apollo Drive, Rosedale, North Shore, Auckland 1311, New Zealand (a division of Pearson New Zealand Ltd.)

Penguin Books (South Africa) (Pty.) Ltd., 24 Sturdee Avenue, Rosebank, Johannesburg 2196, South Africa

Penguin Books Ltd., Registered Offices: 80 Strand, London WC2R 0RL, England

International Standard Book Number: 978-1-59257-658-6
Library of Congress Catalog Card Number: 2007922829

09   08   07   8   7   6   5   4   3   2   1

Interpretation of the printing code: The rightmost number of the first series of numbers is the year of the book's printing; the rightmost number of the second series of numbers is the number of the book's printing. For example, a printing code of 07-1 shows that the first printing occurred in 2007.

Printed in the United States of America

Note: This publication contains the opinions and ideas of its author. It is intended to provide helpful and informative material on the subject matter covered. It is sold with the understanding that the author and publisher are not engaged in rendering professional services in the book. If the reader requires personal assistance or advice, a competent professional should be consulted.

The author and publisher specifically disclaim any responsibility for any liability, loss, or risk, personal or otherwise, which is incurred as a consequence, directly or indirectly, of the use and application of any of the contents of this book.

Most Alpha books are available at special quantity discounts for bulk purchases for sales promotions, premiums, fund-raising, or educational use. Special books, or book excerpts, can also be created to fit specific needs.

For details, write: Special Markets, Alpha Books, 375 Hudson Street, New York, NY 10014.

Publisher: *Marie Butler-Knight*
Editorial Director: *Mike Sanders*
Managing Editor: *Billy Fields*
Acquisitions Editor: *Michele Wells*
Senior Development Editor: *Christy Wagner*
Production Editor: *Megan Douglass*
Copy Editor: *Jennifer Connolly*

Cartoonist: *Shannon Wheeler*
Cover Designer: *Kurt Owens*
Book Designer: *Trina Wurst*
Indexer: *Johnna Vanhoose Dinse*
Layout: *Ayanna Lacey*
Proofreader: *Mary Hunt*

Contents at a Glance

Contents

Introduction

Pizza—how can anyone not like it? What started as an Italian import has become as American as apple pie. When I was young, my family moved from New York to Florida, leaving behind, among other things, New York–style pizza. It took years before we found a place in Florida that could make a halfway decent slice. But you, lucky reader, don't need to wait to find good examples of pizza and panini near you. Even if you live down the street from a good restaurant, with the book in your hands, you have the information you need to make perfect pizza and panini at home. No more delivery fees, and no more take-out.

Panini are a recent phenomenon. At one time in Italy, the term *panini* meant any type of sandwich. But as the Italian influenced moved to the United States, the sandwiches met the grill, and the result was toasted bread encapsulating all sorts of fillings.

The Complete Idiot's Guide to Pizza and Panini helps you bake pizza and grill panini (on your own homemade bread, if you like) like a pro— and even better. In fact, what you make at home will often be better than just about anything you could buy because *you* made it.

You do need some kitchen experience to navigate the world of great homemade pizza and panini, but not much past being able to use a pot or knife safely—you don't need to have ever made bread or pizzas before. In the following pages, I include instructions that walk you through all the preparation steps, along with some fun stuff, too, like the ingredients and equipment you need and the techniques for mixing, kneading, shaping, and baking doughs.

And as you'd expect, there are recipes—nearly 100 of them, many with variations—for pizza, flatbread, and bread dough plus sauce recipes. Also included are recipes for specific pizzas and panini—meat and meatless versions, internationally inspired, even breakfast.

This is a book to use, not just read and put back on the shelf. So sure, check it out and enjoy some of the humor (I keep telling myself I put some in), but also be sure to do some cooking and invite friends and family to join in the repast. Oh, and save me a slice.

How to Use This Book

The best place to start is at the beginning. Check out **Part 1, "Introducing Pizza and Panini,"** if you're not at your most confident in the kitchen. Here you can learn about the basic ingredients and equipment and pick up the fundamental techniques you need for everything in this book.

Part 2, "Starting from Scratch," is a different kind of foundation: recipes. Included are doughs for pizzas, flatbreads, and not-so-flat breads, plus sauces that go together like so many blocks to put together your meal.

Part 3, "It's a Flat, Flat, Flat, Flat World," is devoted to pizza recipes of all types, and **Part 4, "Between a Roll and a Hot Place,"** is full of panini recipes. If a recipe in these pages calls for specific doughs or sauces, I point you to the appropriate chapters.

At the back, I've included a comprehensive glossary—containing all the terminology that has grown up around food.

Extras

Recipes and background on cooking are fine, but sometimes it's nice to have a useful nugget right when it's handy. That why I've included four types of sidebars throughout:

Hot Stuff

Be sure to read these warning boxes for heads-ups of what *not* to do.

Doughfinition

Look to these boxes for a quick definition within easy reach when you need it.

Tips, Please

The hints and tips in these boxes make life easier—all without needing an advanced culinary degree.

Secret Ingredient

For some extra fun—or to impress your friends—check out these culinary oddities and trivia.

Online Bonus

It became clear after writing this book that there was too much to fit into the number of pages planned. Rather than toss perfectly good material, I decided to offer it as a bonus on my website: www.eriksherman.com/pizza. There you'll find descriptions of techniques, photos, and additional recipes—all free for the taking.

Acknowledgments

Thanks to Michele Wells and the other people at Alpha Books who took a chance on a new cookbook author. I knew sending pastries would eventually break down their will.

Special thanks to Cuisinart and Le Creusette, who both sent over panini grill equipment that let me do more than just imagine the crisp exterior of a grilled sandwich. Also thanks to the eating establishments, organizations, and chefs that donated their expertise and even recipes: Arcodoro & Pomodoro Ristorante Italiani (Dallas, Texas), Arpeggio Restaurant (Spring House, Pennsylvania), La Cucina Italiana (New York City), Naples 24 (New York City), Poggio Trattoria (Sausalito, California), Original Pat's King of Steaks (Philadelphia, Pennsylvania), Pomegranate Bistro (Redmond, Washington), and Soleil Bistro (Atlanta, Georgia).

Finally, my family and a number of our friends were all guinea pigs for more pizza and panini than they ever imagined they'd have to eat at a single sitting.

Special Thanks to the Technical Reviewer

The Complete Idiot's Guide to Pizza and Panini was reviewed by an expert who double-checked the accuracy of what you'll learn here, to help us ensure that this book gives you everything you need to know about making great pizza and panini at home. Special thanks are extended to Jeremy Brody.

Trademarks

All terms mentioned in this book that are known to be or are suspected of being trademarks or service marks have been appropriately capitalized. Alpha Books and Penguin Group (USA) Inc. cannot attest to the accuracy of this information. Use of a term in this book should not be regarded as affecting the validity of any trademark or service mark.

Part 1

Introducing Pizza and Panini

In Part 1, we start with a look at the equipment you need to make great-tasting pizza and panini at home, plus cover the techniques you'll use for everything from measuring ingredients to kneading dough and cooking it. If you're already a pro in the kitchen, you might not need all the information in Part 1, but do check it out anyway. You might learn something that makes your kitchen time easier and more fun.

Chapter 1

Your Own Pizza and Panini Joint

In This Chapter

◆ Stocking your pantry

◆ Choosing your operating tools

◆ Fanning the fire

What foods could be more convenient and inconvenient at the same time than pizza and grilled panini? Those discs of sauce, cheese, and other toppings and the hot Italian sandwiches are delicious in their essential simplicity. Nevertheless, if you wanted a pie, or even a slice, that means visiting a restaurant, facing takeout that's gone tepid by the time you get it home, paying a delivery fee on top of the pizza guy's tip, or heaving a frozen disc into the oven. As for those grilled sandwiches, if you didn't have the equipment to make your own, you were pretty much out of luck.

With just a bit of know-how, though, you'll find that these foods are simple to prepare at home, with an authenticity and flavor few restaurants can match. A bit of practice will have you serving up meals with ease and with an international flair closer to these foods' true heritage.

If you want to do everything yourself, I've included recipes for pizza and bread doughs and basic sauces. If you want to save time, you can of course, buy some things ready made, including sauces, ready-made pizza doughs, even ready-to-top crusts. You can also find great bread at a local bakery.

You also need some basic ingredients and equipment on hand to make great pizza and panini. I cover that stuff in this chapter, too.

In the Pantry

Your favorite pizza needs a few ingredients. At the moment, though, I'm only going to talk about dough ingredients and not toppings or sauce. What's this? A sudden aggression against anchovies? Pepperoni pathos? Mozzarella melancholy? Worry not, oh patrons of pizza and panini. It's just practicality. There are too many possible fillings and toppings to keep them all on hand, and you'll be picking up what you need for what you want to make. But because you'll be making dough for everything, those are the ingredients you want tucked away in your pantry.

The Grain Grind

Pizza and panini mean dough, and dough means *flour*. Much flour is made from wheat because it has the *gluten* that traps the gas the *yeast* creates. When you want to mix up the taste and texture, you can with different flours. After all, who would make a Reuben pizza on a white crust?

Secret Ingredient

Flour companies vary the gluten in flours by mixing different amounts of wheat grown in the winter (higher in gluten) and in the spring (lower gluten).

Even when you use other grains, you'll still need wheat flour; otherwise, your dough won't rise. But there's wheat flour and then there's wheat flour. Different types of wheat flour are made by varying how finely they're ground and how much gluten they contain. You're probably used to *all-purpose flour*; it's a good all-around choice with a moderate amount of gluten that you can use for just about everything. But don't stop there. Try *bread flour*. It's high in gluten; the extra amount gives a loaf a lighter texture and more volume plus a bit of chewiness. Then there's *cake flour*, which is finely ground and lower in gluten so you don't find your teeth wrestling with that slice on your plate. You can even get *whole wheat* flour, which adds a nutty taste but rises less than *white flour*.

Flour in other countries can be a lot different. For example, Italians make their doughs, particularly pizza dough, from very finely ground flour that has a soft texture. The best type for baking is *tipo 00 flour*. (You can get this flour at some specialty stores and mail-order locations.) Part of getting a more authentic result in baking at least a real Italian pizza means using Italian tipo 00 flour. Choosing one gets confusing because 00 flour can run from a gluten level even lower than many American cake flours to almost as much gluten as bread flour. Unfortunately, there's no way of telling from the packaging how much gluten the flour contains. In my experience, it's not worth a moment of worry.

Doughfinition

Flour is ground-up grains, mainly wheat for the doughs you'll make in this book. **Gluten** is the protein that gives wheat flour its stretch and texture. You'll typically choose from medium gluten content **all-purpose flour,** high gluten content **bread flour,** low gluten content **cake flour,** and **whole-wheat flour,** which contains the entire wheat grain rather than just the inner parts, as found in **white flours,** like the other flours. Sometimes you might want to incorporate other flours made of oats, rye, buckwheat, or rice. **Tipo 00 flour** is an Italian flour that's finely ground and good for pizza dough.

I've had good results with two types: Antico Molina Caputo (or just Caputo) and Belaria. A 2 kilogram (2.2 pound) package just runs a few dollars, so experimenting is cheap enough. However, you might not enjoy rushing from place to place to find what you need. Luckily, you can get good results by blending the various types of U.S. flour you can find in your local market. In Chapter 4, you'll find a variety of recipes that give you a lighter or chewier dough, depending on what you'd like.

Getting a Rise

If as a kid you ever mixed together flour and water to make dough ornaments or a relief map, you know that what you get is anything but light or even chewy. When making bread, you need something to put in that lift, to create all those fluffy little holes. In short, you need gas. Bread dough rises because of *yeast*, which dine on bits and pieces of the flour and produce a byproduct of carbon dioxide. The yeast has fun and reproduces, creating more yeast and more gas, pushing that dome of dough upward to the top of your bowl.

You can find many kinds of yeast all about you in the air. You can literally start a batch of dough rising by leaving a loose mix of flour and water sitting in a warm place, but it's a gamble and doesn't always work, so it's best to get your yeast at the local market.

Doughfinition

Yeast is a type of tiny organism that chews up flour and burps out carbon dioxide to make the bubbles that cause dough to rise. **Live yeast** comes in blocks, ready to use. **Dried yeast** comes in packets and jars and needs to be dissolved in warm water to come back to life.

Hot Stuff

Some specialty stores, including health food shops and brew-your-own-beer emporiums, might carry brewer's yeast. It can add an interesting flavor when mixed with baking yeast, but on its own it won't make your dough rise.

Most professional bakers and some pizza purists use *live yeast* because it has a stronger rising power and flavor. I prefer *dried yeast.* The live stuff doesn't keep long, and unless you're making so much dough that your friends and family get sick of pizza and panini, you're better off with something that lasts longer. You can purchase dried yeast in packets if you want, but I recommend buying it in a jar because it lasts a long time in your fridge—the best place to keep it. Many of the recipes in this book call for a ½ packet of yeast, or about 1⅛ teaspoons. With a jar, you can measure out the exact amount and then screw the top back on. If you fold over the top of the packet to save it, you know it's going to open up and shower its contents onto the produce below when you close the refrigerator. Messy.

The Salt of the Earth—or Sea

Just about any bread-type dough recipe you see, outside of some well-known exceptions from Tuscany, is going to call for salt. It plays two roles in bread-type doughs. One is flavor, adding a subtle element that you'd be hard-pressed to explain but that you'd notice if was absent. Another role salt plays is yeast control. Given their own way, those little devils will eat and gas, eat and gas, providing runaway yeast population growth and runaway bread expansion. The longer the yeast takes to rise, the more complex a flavor it creates, so you want to exercise some reproductive restraint. Salt slows yeast growth, and so provides an internal break.

You might run across a few different types of salt, including *table salt*, *kosher salt*, and *sea salt*. At times I call for one or the other in these recipes, but for the most part, you can swap them around with no problem.

Doughfinition

Table salt is the ordinary kind you put into the shaker and can buy at the grocery store. **Kosher salt** is coarser and lacks any additives (like iodine). It can have a subtler flavor and doesn't dissolve as fast when sprinkled on food. **Sea salt** comes in flakes that are harvested from the ocean and has a more complex flavor—and more expensive price tag.

Water, Water Everywhere

Three-quarters of the surface of the planet is water, and so is an even larger percentage of you. You'll also find water in cooking and baking—and dough. That's a good thing, too. Imagine what you'd have otherwise. "Mighty fine toasted flour powder you're serving tonight, Martha." No water, no dough.

But people forget that water carries minerals and who knows what else. Different sources provide different results and tastes. At Naples 45, a Manhattan restaurant, Chef Charlie Restivo actually brings in water for baking his praised pizzas from upstate New York—even though Manhattan is known for having good-tasting water. The water he brings in is a harder water, he says, that's more alkaline and similar to the water of Naples, the birthplace of pizza. But for most home cooks, water from the tap works just fine.

Not every place has good-tasting water. I remember growing up in southern Florida and the ... strong presence the liquid had. (I'm reluctant to even call it water.) If the flavor from your local pipes makes you wish for a backyard treatment plant, consider an alternative. You could get a filtration system—we have one for our well-supplied water—or handle the occasional batch of dough with the occasional bottle of spring water.

In-*fat*-uation

A staple of the bread maker's larder is fat. Whether oil or butter, fat adds moisture and an additional flavor component to the final product. Recipes generally call for oil, butter, or shortening. You're going to notice, though, that many of the dough recipes in this book don't call for any type of fat. That's because pizza traditionally is made without it. The pies are generally eaten right out of the oven, so you don't worry about needing moisture to help keep things fresh over time.

Panini, on the other hand, call for bread or rolls, so sometimes it's best to add a little something—typically *olive oil*. Some of recipes in this book also call for cooking a topping or filling in a splash of it. You may have heard talk of *extra-virgin olive oil*. While we might add that to a dough, we won't cook in it. The stuff is far more expensive than the regular olive oil, and when you're dumping it into a pan, you lose the extra-virgin extra taste quality that commands the extra price.

Some dough recipes in Chapter 4 call for butter and *clarified butter*, a traditional ingredient in east Indian cuisine. If you need clarified butter, all you'll do is heat it until the fats separate, but the recipes that call for it explain the process.

> **Doughfinition**
>
> **Olive oil** is a fragrant liquid produced by crushing or pressing olives. **Extra-virgin olive oil** is made from the first pressing of the olives (meaning "regular" olive oil uses the leftovers). Use the fancier stuff when the oil is drizzled over something; otherwise, regular is better. **Clarified butter** has been heated until the solids separate out and any water evaporates. You skim off any solids from the top and then pour the clear liquid off, leaving the milk solids that sink to the bottom.

The Equipment Room

You can buy ingredients as you need them, and the same is true for equipment. There's no reason to start out laying out all sorts of money for things you don't need that badly. At the same time, some appliances and gadgets make life a whole lot easier—and a few are just a lot of fun.

Board Already

You're going to need someplace to work the dough—even if you don't do everything by hand. (Hang on for that until the next section.) Your workspace should be big enough—about 1½ to 2 feet because you'll be rolling and flattening out the pizza dough almost 1 foot in every direction.

A clear space on a kitchen counter will do just fine, although a pastry board is my preference. I can pull it out and move it around as necessary, setting up my workspace on a counter or a table, dodging other food preparation and members of my family as they stake out various parts of the kitchen. I also protect other surfaces in the kitchen and avoid the possibility of cross-contamination from working on a surface that has previous held raw meat or fish.

Boards come in a variety of materials, from wood to thin plastic sheets you can roll up for easier storage. I use a solid marble board. The surface is cool, which helps keep dough easy to work, it doesn't scratch or nick, and it won't absorb flour or liquid. Unfortunately, the weight when I'm getting it in and out of the cabinet can be a big drawback. A wooden pastry board is a good compromise—less weight, works great—just don't use it as a cutting board, too. You want a smooth surface, not one covered with scratches and cuts from knives.

> **Tips, Please**
>
> The weight of a marble board keeps it in place pretty well. If you're using a wooden board and find that it slips about as you work, wet a cloth kitchen towel, wring out the extra liquid, set it on the counter, and put the board on top. You shouldn't have any more problems with sliding.

Let's Go *Bowl*-ing

You'll need a good-size bowl for both mixing your dough and letting the yeast get to work and double in size. A metal bowl should be
fine; it's what I use. A large crockery bowl would also be good. Avoid
a wooden bowl for making dough. Over time, you run the risk of
the moisture in the dough turning the bowl into a bacterial breeding
ground. And that's one "topping" you just don't want.

A Weighty Consideration

Although many of the measurements in this book are in volume, at
times, nothing beats a kitchen scale. Some ingredients don't lend them-
selves to counting slices or measuring some number of cups.

I just switched to a digital scale and am not looking back to the
old spring models. You get good accuracy, and the numeric readout is
far less ambiguous.

All Mixed Up

When you make dough for pizza or bread, you must mix and knead.
You can blend the ingredients with a large wooden spoon and then
knead the dough by hand (see Chapter 3). Or you can opt for some
mechanical help. I like using a *stand
mixer* because the kneading is stronger and better and can go on while I
continue other preparations. A regular portable hand mixer isn't a substitute and can't knead dough at all.

A *food processor* can also be an
aid but presents a slight problem
because it can get the dough too hot.
There are some tricks to deal with
this, though, and I get into them in
Chapter 3.

> **Doughfinition**
>
> A **stand mixer** sits atop
> a counter or table and
> mixes, whips, and kneads. A
> powerful motor moves the unit's
> attachments through whatever
> needs the workout. A **food
> processor** is a container with
> changeable blades at the
> bottom that can mix, cut, and
> knead.

Handling Yourself—and the Dough

Even when you use your hands, some tools are a must. *Dough scrapers* let you work more easily with the sticky doughs you'll often be using. The plastic variety are pretty cheap, and they're too useful not to have one or two around.

Peels are also good to have. They come with handles of vary-ing lengths and may have wood or metal blades. You're best off with two. The wood-blade ones are good for sliding formed dough that doesn't need a pan into an oven, while the metal blades more easily slip under the baked good to remove it from the oven.

Doughfinition

A **dough scraper** is a metal or plastic rectangu-lar blade that lets you scrape dough off a work surface. A **peel** is handle with a flat blade at one end you can use to get bread and pizza in and out of the oven.

If you don't want to spend money on peels, you can use a thin cutting board or a cookie sheet to slide something into the oven and a spatula to take it out when it's done. However, the peels do work bet-ter. For a long time, I split the difference and used a wooden peel to get something into the oven and a spatula (or two) to get it out.

A good-size rolling pin isn't as necessary as you might think. You'll generally be forming the pizzas, rolls, and breads with your hands. But there are times that the pin is handy in flattening out a clump of dough.

Kitchen Kut-Up

You will need to cut dough, and a kitchen knife—or any other type you have around—can work. Some types of breads or rolls for panini might need to have their tops sliced or marked before you put them into the oven, and you really want a thin sharp blade for this. A boning or par-ing knife can do, or you can get a special type of tool built for scoring the dough. It's a handle that holds a razor blade and lets you safely score the dough without doing the same to your fingers.

Ah, but the cutting doesn't end there. When pizzas come out of the oven, they need to be cut into slices. (You really weren't going to eat the whole thing by yourself, were you?) You'll see some people swear by kitchen shears; others say you need one of those handles with a rotary blade like you see in some pizzerias; still others like a big kitchen knife. It's all personal preference and doesn't matter. I wouldn't go the shears route myself, as that means holding the pizza up with one hand and getting the other way too close to that molten cheese. I have a rotary cutter and use it when it hasn't gone missing. Otherwise, it's the big knife method for me.

> **Tips, Please**
>
> Some kitchen tools are versatile. When working with dough, I usually already have a scraper in my hand. When it's time to divide the dough into pieces, I push down through it with the edge of the scraper. There's one fewer thing to wash later.

The Third Degree

You also want to know where everything is in terms of temperature. Have a separate oven thermometer so you can see how far off the oven temperature really is from where you set the dial so you can get the right amount of heat and your bread comes out right. When it's time for pizzas, the worry is less because you'll turn your oven up all the way, and like it or not, that's as hot as it can get.

You might find it useful to have an instant-read pocket thermometer. Although real bakers often calculate all the temperatures of all the ingredients to help achieve the optimum conditions, that's not necessary for the home pizzaiolo. But there will be the odd time an instant-read thermometer comes in handy, like when you want to be sure your hot tap water is between 105°F and 110°F so the yeast will dissolve and not wither and die.

Hot Stuff

Eventually, you need to bake what you've so carefully made. Chances are you're not going to be investing the money or time in building a wood-fired oven. (Too bad—I was going to ask if I could come over and try it.) Yet thinking about a wood oven is a good idea, because it's ideal for baking what we're making with a flat surface that helps develop the crust and a temperature running between 700°F and 800°F. That makes the top setting on your home oven look like a trip to the Arctic.

Secret Ingredient

If you really want your own wood oven, companies build them and even sell kits you can assemble at home.

There's nothing we can do to make the oven hotter, but we can create a better cooking surface. One possibility is a commercially available pizza stone. A better and more economic choice is to line one of your oven shelves with unglazed ceramic tile. An entire rack's worth will probably cost less than a pizza stone and you'll have lots more baking room. One advantage of the stone is that you can easily take it out of the oven when you don't need it. You can get the tiles out, too, although you'll need a place to keep them stacked until they're needed again. Some people line a big sheet pan with tiles and slide the assembly in for baking and out when it's unnecessary.

Notice I haven't mentioned pans; you don't need 'em for pizzas, unless you hanker for making your own Chicago-style deep-dish pizza. Here a pan is a must. You can go for a blackened metal pan, which helps develop the crust. If you don't have one, don't worry—experiment with a regular pie pan or a rectangular baking pan, for that matter. It's pizza—how bad can it possibly be?

Where pans come in handy is with breads. Some breads you make are free-form, but others—sandwich loaves, for example—require a *loaf pan*.

If you get bored with baking pizza in the oven, you might consider outdoor grilling. You can either try baking one right on the grill or you can put a pizza stone on the grill first and let it heat up. In either case, be sure you have a top for the grill because you want heat to surround the pizza. Use a gas grill or, for a twist, an old-fashioned kettle-style grill.

Doughfinition

A **loaf pan** is a rectangular form that keeps a loaf of bread in a regular symmetrical shape, like sandwich types you'd find in a grocery store.

For panini, even after the bread or rolls are baked, you still need to grill the sandwich. You can do this on an outdoor or indoor grill with something to press the panino firmly onto the grill. A cast-iron weight with an insulating handle, like a bacon or sandwich press, is ideal.

Tips, Please _____
With a kettle grill and a pizza stone, you can actually stoke a hot wood fire and get the smokiness an indoor oven is going to miss. Or compromise between wood and briquettes and use real charcoal.

If you don't have a grill or don't feel like firing it up, use a cast-iron grill, which is really a pan that has ridges on the inside. They give the grill marks while keeping the sandwich up above the butter or oil you'll use. Almost makes it sound earthy-crunchy, doesn't it?

The Least You Need to Know

◆ Keep a variety of dough ingredients in your pantry and you'll be ready to spin a pie in no time.

◆ A 1½- to 2-foot-square workspace is best for working dough.

◆ Stand mixers are handy but not required.

◆ Dough scrapers are your best friend when it comes to handling and cutting the dough.

◆ A pizza stone or unglazed ceramic tile make great baking surfaces.

A Chapter You Knead to Read

In This Chapter

- ◆ Basic dough-making steps
- ◆ Working with yeast
- ◆ Mixing and kneading dough
- ◆ Cooking tips

You can't get anywhere making pizzas or panini without dough—the gooey type, that is. Although recipes vary, there are actually only a few techniques at the basis of them all. Learn these, and you'll be able to make any dough. The more you know about the basic techniques, the more you'll see that the differences among pizza and panini recipes are pretty minor, and the more confidence you'll have.

In this chapter, we go from getting the dough ready to shaping it and cooking it, with a nod to some shortcuts to save time and energy. You even learn how to put off some stages of preparing the dough so it works around your schedule instead of the other way around.

The Dough, Re, Mi

Let's start with the basics. Making the dough takes a few easy steps:

1. Dissolve the yeast in the water.

2. Mix together the flour and salt. Include the sugar if there is any.

3. Mix the water with the fat.

4. Combine the water mixture with the flour mixture.

5. Knead the dough and let it rise.

6. Cut the dough into portions and shape.

7. Let dough rise again.

8. Bake.

Once you get the hang of making one kind of dough, you're most of the way to making any other. But no matter what dough you're making, in addition to ingredients, you need a few other tools:

◆ Measuring cups

◆ Measuring spoons

◆ A pastry board or work surface

◆ A knife to cut the dough

◆ A scraper

◆ A large bowl to mix the dough and let it rise

◆ A large wooden spoon

◆ Plastic wrap

◆ A timer

◆ A stand mixer or food processor (optional)

Sound Familiar?

After reading a number of dough recipes, you'll find that they are often similar. That's because nature—and human tastes—take a hand in food science. For example, you need about 1 teaspoon salt for every 3 cups flour to get the right taste. You might add a little more or less, but it will be in the ballpark.

There's one big difference between the pizza and bread doughs. The former is nothing but flour, salt, water, and yeast. The bread and roll recipes, however, often contain some fat to help keep them moist after baking and may include sugar or other ingredients as well. Even so, for the most part, you still use the same basic steps.

Yeast Feast

If you have some bread-baking experience, many of the recipes in this book might seem to have too little yeast. All that does is make the dough take a little bit longer to rise, which gives the yeast a chance to create more flavor. If you're pressed for time, you can safely double the yeast to get it to rise faster. These recipes generally call for ½ a packet, or 1⅛ teaspoons, so you don't have to deal with having odd amounts like a ⅕ package left over. (And as I mentioned in Chapter 1, getting a jar of yeast instead of packets lets you measure out what you need.)

If use dried yeast, you need to dissolve it in liquid between roughly 105°F and 110°F. The easiest way to do this is to take the liquid for recipe, get it to the right temperature range, sprinkle the yeast over the top, wait a minute, and then stir the combination with a whisk or fork.

If your yeast is out of date but you don't have time to go get new, follow the steps in a dough recipe through dissolving the dried yeast in the liquid and then wait 5 to 10 minutes. If you see bubbles, you're in business. If not, you've minimized your waste and only need to toss the water and the useless yeast.

Secret Ingredient

Notice that unlike in many bread recipes, in this book, I don't call for using only part of the liquid to dissolve the yeast, add no sugar to the yeast and water, and don't instruct you to wait 10 minutes or so for the mix to get frothy. There's not even a call to scald any milk that may be included. Some of these steps have been handed down from one recipe to the next because at one time they were necessary. In the past, yeast was less reliable than today, and waiting for it to bubble was called *proofing*—which meant you were proving that the batch of yeast was still good.

A Measure of Flour

In any bread recipe, you need just the right amount of flour. Too little, and the dough is soupy; too much, and you have resistant plaster. Unfortunately, the little particles of flour can move aside and allow air between them, making volume measurements like cups uncertain. Shake the flour some, the air comes out, and the flour level settles. A cup of well-packed flour will contain more than an equal measure of fully aerated flour. Professional bakers and European cookbooks generally solve this problem by specifying amounts in weight. But most home cooks have become used to volume measure, so in this book, I list the measurements in volume whenever possible.

To avoid ambiguity in measure as much as possible, the recipes in this book assume you have air in the flour. The classic way of doing this is to first sift flour onto a piece of wax paper and then spoon the now-aerated flour into your measuring device. And because the remaining flour is on the wax paper, it's easy to pick up the lot and tip it back into its canister. Although that works, here's what I do: keep the flour in an air-tight canister I give a few shakes to before measuring my flour. That mixes the air into the flour pretty well without messing up a sifter.

Hot Stuff

If you go the shaking-the-flour-in-the-canister route, be *sure* the lid is fastened before shaking, else you have the experience I once enjoyed of the lid opening and the flour flying. Not a pretty sight. Plus, you lose far more time in cleaning than you saved in not sifting.

You'll also notice that every recipe in this book gives a range of flour to use. Not only can flour incorporate more or less air, making measurement uncertain, but it can absorb moisture from the air so the dough requires less liquid, meaning you need a little more to match the wet ingredients. Even humidity changes can affect how much flour you need on any given day. Always mix in the smaller amount of flour listed and only add as much as you need for the right dough texture—more on this shortly.

Mix and Knead with Speed

With dough comes mixing and kneading. Mixing combines the wet ingredients with the dry. Then you knead the dough to further distribute all the ingredients for a uniform batch of dough and also to develop the gluten so the dough will rise, making the final baked good lighter and more tender.

Mix It Up

When the dry ingredients and the wet ingredients are well mixed together—it should only take a couple minutes at most—check out the dough. Depending on the type of dough, you'll see and feel different things.

Doughs for pizza and certain breads like *ciabatta* (*chyah-BAH-tah*) contain a lot of water, which turns into steam and helps make the airy pockets found in the final baked product. The dough for these is going to be sticky. If you touch it and pull your hand away, strands will cling. When you bake these doughs, the inside texture, or *crumb*, is open, with large holes and pockets. Other baked goods, like sandwich breads, have a finer crumb. Their doughs are drier and should come away from the sides of the mixing bowl but stick only slightly to your hand.

Doughfinition

Ciabatta is a type of rustic bread found in Italy.
Crumb is the texture of the inside of bread.

If a dough is too wet, add flour 1 tablespoon at a time, mixing more after each addition. If the dough is too dry, add 1 teaspoon of water at a time and keep mixing.

People Who Knead Pizza ...

When everything is mixed and the texture is right, you're ready to knead. This is actually an easy process:

1. Turn the dough out of the mixing bowl and onto a floured work surface.

> **Tips, Please**
>
> Kneading dough can be messy work. I knead the dough with one hand and keep a dough scraper in my free hand. If the dough sticks to the board, I have the scraper handy to loosen it, and if I need to add flour, I don't drag globs of goo into my supply. I either lightly dust my free hand with flour if the dough is a drier one, or rub a little oil on it if the dough is sticky so I don't have clumps sticking to my skin.

2. With your free hand, grasp the far edge of the dough, lift it, and fold it back to meet the near edge.

3. Put the heel of your hand against the top of the mass of dough and push down and away from you. You aren't sliding the dough so much as spreading it forward.

4. Turn the mass of dough ⅛ turn (using the scraper if necessary to free it from the work surface), go back to step 3, and repeat.

> **Secret Ingredient**
>
> To see photos of the kneading process and what the doughs should look like, go to the food section of my website, www.eriksherman.com/pizza.

Knead doughs for the airy-textured breads and pizzas, those with the wet and sticky doughs, about 5 minutes. For the finer-textured breads, knead about 8 to 10 minutes—long enough for the dough to properly develop but not enough to make your arm feel like it's going to fall off. This is a great way to take out frustration with your day. You can occasionally take the entire mass of dough, lift it into the air, and slam it down onto the work surface—which helps develop the texture.

Mechanized Kneading

There's an easier way to knead: use a machine. I mentioned stand mixers and food processors in Chapter 2. When making a fine-crumb bread dough, the former is my personal favorite. Here are the steps for using a stand mixer; I'm using a KitchenAid as an example; other makes will have different but similar ways of operating:

1. Put the dry ingredients into the mixer bowl and attach the flat mixing paddle.

2. Place the bowl on the mixer and raise it into place. Turn on the mixer to the lowest speed to stir. Add the water and yeast combination. Usually a minute of mixing is all that's necessary.

3. Lower the bowl and remove and clean the paddle, putting any extra dough back into the bowl.

4. Attach the dough hook and raise the bowl. Turn on the mixer to the lowest speed for about 5 minutes for the airier doughs and about 8 for the finer crumbs.

Pay close attention to the time, as it is possible to over knead. At the end of the kneading, check the texture of the dough. It should appear as it would after hand-kneading (see the preceding "People Who Knead Pizza ..." section).

Using a food processor is trickier because the high blade speed creates a lot of heat that can start killing off the yeast. Here's how to combat this problem with any of the dough recipes:

1. Divide the water called for in the recipe into two equal parts. One should be in the 105°F to 110°F range. The other should be ice cold (chilled before measuring).

2. Dissolve the yeast in the warm water. If a recipe calls for adding oil, mix it with the warm water after the yeast is dissolved.

3. When the recipe calls for placing the dry ingredients into a bowl, put them into the bowl of the food processor with the steel blade.

4. When the direction calls for mixing the water and dry ingredients, put the cover on the food processor. Mix the cold water with the warm water mixture out of the food processor.

5. Start the food processor blade. Open the feed tube and slowly add the water. When the dough starts to collect on top of the blade, turn off the food processor.

6. Take off the cover and remove the metal blade. Replace it with the plastic kneading blade. Replace the top.

7. Run the food processor for 3 minutes. Stop, remove the top, and check the texture as before.

By adding the cold water, you help moderate the temperature. Because the blades spin so quickly, you don't need much time for mixing or kneading.

Getting a Rise

After you've kneaded the bread, it's time to lightly coat a bowl with oil, put the dough in the bowl, cover the bowl with plastic wrap, and let the dough sit and rise. This helps the dough develop its yeast and the texture.

Depending on the type of dough, you'll use a different pattern of rising. Sometimes you let the dough double in size once. Sometimes you let it rise part way, press out the gas that's built up inside, and then let it rise again. Sometimes you let dough rise so much that it triples in size and then starts to deflate again. Each dough recipe comes with instructions for how and when to let the dough rise.

Tips, Please

When you let the dough double in size, here's a good way to see if it's finished: stick two fingers about an inch or so into the dough and then pull them out. If the dough has risen enough, the holes your fingers made will remain. If the dough springs back, whether slowly or quickly, it still has some time to go.

Folding Dough

When the dough has risen enough, you sometimes have to remove the gas from the dough. In many dough recipes that's called "punching down." Here's a way of deflating the dough that makes a better texture:

1. Turn out the dough onto a well-floured work surface.

2. Lift up the far edge of the dough, bring it to the middle of the dough, and then press down the flap to squeeze out the gas. Lift the near edge of the dough, bring it to the middle, and then press down that flap to push out the gas. Be careful not to add more flour to the top of the dough.

3. In a similar manner, bring the right and left edges in to the middle and press down to remove the gas.

4. Lift the dough, turn it over in your hands, and brush the flour from the part of the dough that had been on the work surface.

5. If you need to let the dough rise again, place it back in the bowl with the edges that you folded facing down into the bowl. Remember to replace the plastic loosely over the top of the bowl.

Tips, Please

Instead of deflating the dough on the work surface, I've found that I can do more or less the same thing in a bowl. You don't have to think about which side of the dough is facing up and you make less mess.

Letting dough rise can play havoc with your schedule if you have places to go and people to see—you're pretty much stuck in and around your home until it's ready. For some breathing room, do the following after the dough is kneaded and before it has risen:

1. Form the dough into a ball.

2. Lightly oil one side of a square of plastic wrap large enough to wrap around the ball.

3. Loosely wrap the plastic around the dough (oil side touching the dough), and place it in the refrigerator.

You now have a good 6 to 10 hours at your fingertips, because in the cold refrigerator, the dough rises very slowly. When you get back and can finish cooking, take the dough out of the fridge and let it warm and finish rising.

Shape It Up

At some point with either pizza or bread, you have to shape what you'll be eating. Each one has a different technique. Pizza, obviously, will be flat. But while it's often prepared round, some variations are prepared as rectangles. As for breads, they can be freeform ovals or rounds baked directly on a stone, or shaped to fit into a loaf pan. (I discuss shaping dough later in the book.)

Pie-Eyed

The simplest way to shape pizza is to flatten the ball of dough out on a floured surface until you have a disc. Begin by pushing down on the dough ball with your fingertips, starting in the center and working out, until the dough is about $\frac{1}{8}$-inch thick and about the diameter the dough recipe says you'll get—more or less.

When working from the center, you'll eventually get a build-up of dough at the edge that's about twice as thick as everywhere else. That's exactly what you want, as it creates a crust wall that helps keep the ingredients on the pizza and off the bottom of the oven. Toppings, including sauce, only go up to that edge and not onto it.

Feeling adventurous? Once you have the dough flattened, you can try stretching it over the backs of your hands. Put your hands, knuckles up, under the dough and slightly move your hands up and away from each other, stretching the dough. Careful because as the dough gets thinner, tearing it by accident becomes easier. For the highest in culinary daredevilry, when that dough is sitting on the back of your hands, toss it up flat into the air while turning your hands in a circle.

> **Secret Ingredient**
> For some photos of adventures in dough-tossing, go to my website, www.eriksherman.com/pizza.

Yes, your pizza is flying through the air. The technique does help stretch the dough out some, but more important, it's fun and impressive to those who haven't done it.

Loafing Around

When making bread, you have various choices of loaf shape. With the more rustic types, like ciabatta, you don't form a loaf so much as keep it from flopping about. After the last rising in the bowl, you dump the dough out onto a heavily floured board, at which point you divide it into rectangular shapes and bake them. Simple enough.

Other breads take more handling. You can form them into oval loaves, like Italian breads, or you can make a traditional sandwich-style loaf in a loaf pan. When you use a loaf pan, here's how to shape the dough:

1. Place the dough on a lightly floured work surface and flatten it into a rectangle, with the long edges running left and right in front of you.

2. Lift and bring the right and left sides to meet in the middle of the loaf, pressing these edges down with your fingertips.

3. Fold the two halves of the loaf together, like closing a book. Press the free edges to seal them together. The dough should be in the rough shape of a cylinder.

Tips, Please

Use a cooking spray or oil mister to quickly and cleanly grease the pan.

4. Pinch closed the open ends of the cylinder and then roll the cylinder on your work space, stretching it as you do so to make the loaf longer. Stop when it fits snugly into the loaf pan.

Grease the inside of the loaf pan and place the dough, long seam side down, into the pan.

The Heat Is On

The big trick in baking pizza or even bread is using either unglazed ceramic tile or a pizza stone (remember those from Chapter 1?). You should have had the store providing you with the tile cut to fit in a pan, and it's that pan that goes into the oven on a rack set in the middle. The pizza stone would go in the same place.

Put a sturdy roasting pan on the floor of the oven, close the door, and preheat the oven to the temperature required by the recipe. It will take at least a $\frac{1}{2}$ hour to preheat the oven adequately. (I usually let it heat 45 minutes to an hour.) In the meantime, you can shape the pizzas and get your toppings ready.

Getting Steamed

One feature that makes professional ovens different from what we have at home is that bakers can inject steam into the closed oven. The hot moisture helps the crust develop. You aren't going to have that feature on your home oven, even if it is one of those big, fancy ones.

Remember that roasting pan in the bottom of the oven? Here's where it comes in. A few minutes before you're ready to cook, bring a pot of water to a boil. When you open the oven and slide in the pizza or bread, don an oven glove, pull out that pan on the floor of the oven, pour 1 cup boiling water into it, push the pan back in, and close the door. The boiling water provides steam, and the preheated pan keeps the bubbles coming.

Hands Off!

We have one hurdle to go: if you're not using a pan, how do you get the pizza onto the tiles or stone? If you remember the Chapter 2 discussion of peels, here's where it becomes very *appeeling*.

Tips, Please

Even with heavy corn-meal, the dough occasionally sticks to the peel, particularly if you let it sit for any amount of time. When that happens, use a series of short jerks until the dough freely slips back and forth. Now you're ready for the big slide.

When you shape the pizza or a loaf of bread not in a pan, heavily cover the peel's blade with cornmeal before putting the pizza or bread on the peel. The trick to getting the dough off the peel and onto the stone is to move it forward and suddenly jerk it back, leaving the dough where the peel was up until a second before.

It sounds harder than it is, and this is a skill best learned before you actually have to employ it.

Is It Getting Hot in Here?

The other major technique for baking pizzas, in particular, is a hot oven. No, make that a *really hot* oven, as in at least 200°F more than what you have at home. So we make do by setting the oven at 500°F for pizzas. (Bread baking temperatures run anywhere from about 350°F to 425°F.) But while that makes the pizza cook within 10 minutes, sometimes cheese can take a beating, melting so much that it seems to disappear.

You've got two solutions to the disappearing cheese problem. One is to get a better quality of cheese, at least a better quality of mozzarella. According to what I understand from professional pizza chefs, if you use a top grade like mozzarella di bufala, the cheese won't brown and burn. If you can't find or can't afford mozzarella di bufala, or if you're using a recipe that calls for a different type of cheese, here's another idea:

1. Form the pizza as usual, and place it on the peel.

2. Prick the surface lightly with a fork without pushing the tines all the way through the dough.

3. Slide the naked pizza into the hot oven, and bake at 500° for about 2 minutes. It won't be brown, but it will have firmed up.

4. Use a metal peel or a spatula to coax it out and put it on a heat-proof surface.

5. Add your toppings, and send the pizza back into the oven to finish baking.

> **Tips, Please**
>
> When baking bread, use an oven thermometer to verify the temperature settings. If it's off, adjust the temperature appropriately. For example, if the thermometer reads 25° hotter than the setting, set the temperature for 25° cooler than what you want.

Your toppings will be done and the cheese should remain in fine shape. If not, then the next time you make a pizza, give the dough 3 minutes on its own. That's no half-baked idea!

Pressing Matters

Compared with pizzas, panini are easy to cook. You assemble the sandwiches, slather the outer faces with something such as butter or oil to help the cooking process, pop them onto a grill, and press. Pressing helps ensure good contact with the grilling surface as well as even browning.

Secret Ingredient

There are two aesthetic schools on grilling: ridges or flat. My choice is ridges, which I sometimes vary by turning the sandwich 45 degrees when it's halfway cooked. That produces an attractive diamond pattern on the bread. Ridges also help keep the bread above any extra fat, so I suppose technically it's healthier. However, I'll try not to let that deter me.

To make it even easier, you've got choices for what you can use to grill the sandwich:

◆ A self-contained electric unit

◆ The stovetop

◆ A grill

The first is one of those sandwich grills that clamps down with a vengeance and cooks both sides of the panino at once. The cooking surfaces are generally nonstick, so that's easy. A number of manufacturers make such grills; I've used one from Cuisinart with great success.

Stovetop cooking requires a pan and a weight. I use a matched pair from Le Creuset. The cast iron holds the heat and yet the porcelain cleans easily enough. I can fit a couple sandwiches and also have the versatility to grill other items that might not fit nicely or easily between an electric unit's Jaws of Grilling. The downside with stovetop grilling is that it takes longer to cook because you have to flip the sandwich when the first side is done.

If you've got outdoor cooking weather, or if you are one of
those people with a grill on the
stovetop, then by all means, use
it. You'll need a weight, either
designed and bought specially for
the purpose or improvised out of
what you already have at home.
Just be sure to spray some oil on
the grilling surface before you put
it in place to help the sandwich
release.

Tips, Please

If you don't want to spend
money just use a fry pan
or griddle for the grill and
virtually anything—including
a medium saucepan half-full
of water—for the weight. A
nonstick pan or griddle is the
least-vexing choice.

Finally, don't overdo the sandwich filling. Not only do you want
everything to fit within the grill, but you want to minimize the chance
of any ingredients escaping.

Now that you know how to handle dough, let's try your skills on
some pizza and flatbread recipes in the next chapter.

The Least You Need to Know

◆ The same basic techniques work for virtually any bread or pizza
dough.

◆ You may have to adjust the total amount of flour, which is why the
recipes in the following chapters have ranges.

◆ A pan of boiling water set in the bottom of the oven can help
develop crust.

◆ Turn the heat up when baking a pizza. You want it H-O-T.

◆ Don't overfill panini, or you're sure to have a mess on your
hands—literally.

Part 2

Starting from Scratch

They say fresh is best, and that holds true with pizza and panini. Making them from scratch is the best way to enjoy pizza and panini. With that in mind, turn the page. In Part 2, you get recipes for pizza and panini doughs—some of which might really pleasantly surprise you. I also give you a chapter of essential sauce recipes to spread on top.

3

Flat Foundations: Pizza and Flatbread Doughs

In This Chapter

- ◆ Recipes for basic doughs
- ◆ Adding some variety with mixed-grain doughs
- ◆ Mmm … real sour dough

It's time to make dough. Most pizza doughs are straightforward to make. The sourdoughs are a bit more complex, but then, what is life without a little challenge? Even there, the only real hard part is planning ahead and waiting.

If you haven't done much work with yeast doughs before, review Chapter 2 for making and handling techniques. If you have, feel free to plunge ahead. Or if you want, you can buy premade dough from your grocery store or pizzeria, or even get flatbreads and crusts from supermarkets or bakeries and add the toppings.

> **Tips, Please** _____
>
> This chapter's recipes make enough dough for two pizzas or flatbreads. If that's too much, lightly oil the inside of a resealable plastic bag, put the extra dough in, squeeze out the air, and close the bag. You can now put the bag of dough into the freezer for up to a month. To use it, take the bag out of the freezer and put it into the refrigerator 24 hours before you plan to use it.

A Note on Sours

I've included two sour recipes in this chapter—White Sour and Rye Sour. Neither is a dough in and of itself. Instead, both offer a jumpstart on getting a naturally fermented taste into your baking. I've seen devotees of the flavor add it to almost anything, including pancakes.

You're unlikely to use all of a batch at one time, so put the extra into a glass jar, top with ⅛ inch water, and keep it in the refrigerator. Every few days, stir it down and add a new cover of water. Once every 2 weeks, dump ½ sour and add an equal volume of water and flour mixed in equal parts. For example, if you have 1 cup sour, toss ½, whisk together ¼ cup water and ¼ cup flour, and add that combination to the sour, mixing them together. Add ⅛ inch water, and pop it back into the fridge. If the top of the sour gets discolored, pour off the water, skim off the discolored part, and replace the water top.

> **Secret Ingredient** _____
>
> The doughs in this chapter are the foundation—literally—for the panini and pizza recipes in the rest of the book. However, don't get stuck in a rut. If a recipe calls for a wheat crust and you want to substitute oatmeal, give your creativity a chance.

If you want more sour than you have in the refrigerator, take it out, let it warm up, and then start feeding it in stages as happens in the following recipe, at each stage adding an equal volume of water and flour mixed 50-50.

Note: All the prep times listed for the following recipes (save the sours) include the rise time and sometimes the soak time.

Pizza Dough I

This is a soft dough somewhat similar to the results you'd get with Italian flour.

1⅛ tsp. dried instant yeast (½ packet)

1⅜ cups 105°F to 110°F water

3 to 3¾ cups cake flour

¼ cup bread flour

1¼ tsp. salt

1 tsp. vegetable oil

Yield: 2 (10-inch) pizzas

Prep time:
3 hours

Serving size:
⅓ pizza

1. In a small bowl or measuring cup, add yeast to water and stir until dissolved.

2. In a large bowl, combine 3 cups cake flour, bread flour, and salt, and mix thoroughly with a wooden spoon. Add water and yeast mixture to the bowl, and mix until all ingredients are combined and strands of dough still cling to the sides of the bowl.

3. Sprinkle some bread flour on your work surface, place dough on the surface, and knead dough for 8 minutes. Add additional cake flour, 1 tablespoon at a time, as necessary so dough holds together and you can knead it but it still remains very soft and sticky.

4. Add oil to the empty bowl, and swirl the bowl to coat the inside. Don't worry if there's a little oil left in the bottom of the bowl. Return dough to the bowl, and turn dough to coat with oil. Cover the bowl with plastic wrap, and let dough double in volume.

5. When dough has doubled in volume, turn out onto a floured work surface and fold to deflate. Divide dough into two parts, and form each into a ball. Lightly oil two pieces of plastic wrap, each large enough to cover one ball, and loosely cover each ball, oil side in. Allow dough to double in volume.

6. Gently deflate balls, and form each into a 10-inch pizza. Add toppings and bake according to the recipe directions.

Variations: For **Pizza Dough II,** replace cake and bread flours with 3 to
3¾ cups Italian tipo 00 flour. For **Sweet Pizza Dough,** reduce water to 1¼
cups and add ½ cup honey.

Secret Ingredient

Many recipes say that bread must rise in a warm spot, but that isn't
true. So long as you've got the bread at room temperature, it will
rise, though more slowly the cooler the spot.

Pizza Dough III

Try this dough when you want a pizza with a breadier texture.

1⅛ tsp. dried instant yeast (½ packet)

1⅜ cups 105°F to 110°F water

2 or 3 cups bread flour

1 cup cake flour

1¼ tsp. salt

1 tsp. vegetable oil

Yield: 2 (10-inch) pizzas

Prep time:
3 hours

Serving size:
⅓ pizza

1. In a small bowl, add yeast to water and stir until dissolved.

2. In a large bowl, combine 2 cups bread flour, cake flour, and salt, mix thoroughly with a wooden spoon. Add water and yeast mixture to the bowl, and mix until all ingredients are combined and strands of dough still cling to the sides of the bowl.

3. Sprinkle some bread flour on your work surface, place dough on the surface, and knead dough for 8 minutes. Add additional cake flour, 2 tablespoons at a time, as necessary so dough holds together and you can knead it but it still remains very soft and sticky.

4. Add oil to the empty bowl, and swirl the bowl to coat the inside. Don't worry if there's a little oil left in the bottom of the bowl. Return dough to the bowl, and turn dough to coat with oil. Cover the bowl with plastic wrap, and let dough double in volume.

5. When dough has doubled in volume, turn out onto a floured work surface and fold to deflate. Divide dough into two parts, and form each into a ball. Lightly oil two pieces of plastic wrap, each large enough to cover one ball, and loosely cover each ball, oil side in. Allow dough to double in volume.

6. Gently deflate balls, and form each into a 10-inch pizza. Add toppings and bake according to the recipe directions.

Variations: For **Whole-Wheat Pizza Dough,** replace cake flour with 1⅓ cups whole-wheat flour and use 1½ teaspoons salt instead of 1¼ teaspoons.

For **Buckwheat Pizza Dough,** replace cake flour with 1⅓ cups buckwheat flour and use 1½ teaspoons salt instead of 1¼ teaspoons. For **Rye Pizza Dough,** replace cake flour with 1⅓ cups rye flour, use 1½ teaspoons salt instead of 1¼ teaspoons, and add 1 teaspoon ground caraway seed to flour in step 2.

Tips, Please

If the bread flour makes the dough more difficult to work, put it in the refrigerator for ½ hour and then shape it.

Focaccia

This Italian flatbread can be the basis for toppings, or you can cut a square horizontally down the middle to hold panino fillings. It's even great on its own.

1⅛ tsp. dried instant yeast (½ packet)

1¾ cups 105°F to 110°F water

4 or 5 cups all-purpose flour

1¼ tsp. salt

¼ cup plus 1 TB. extra-virgin olive oil

1 tsp. vegetable oil

1 tsp. kosher salt

2 tsp. dried rosemary

Yield: 8 pieces
Prep time:
3 hours
Cook time:
25 minutes
Serving size:
1 piece

1. In a small bowl, add yeast to water and stir until dissolved.

2. In a large bowl, combine 4 cups flour and salt, and mix thoroughly with a wooden spoon. Add water and yeast mixture and ¼ cup extra-virgin olive oil to the bowl. Mix until all ingredients are combined and strands of dough still cling to the sides of the bowl.

3. Sprinkle some flour on your work surface, place dough on the surface, and knead dough for 8 minutes. Add additional flour, 2 tablespoons at a time, as necessary so dough holds together and you can knead it but it still remains very soft and sticky.

4. Add vegetable oil to the empty bowl, and swirl the bowl to coat the inside. Don't worry if there's a little oil left in the bottom of the bowl. Return dough to the bowl, and turn dough to coat with oil. Cover bowl with plastic wrap, and let dough double in volume.

5. When dough has doubled in volume, turn out onto a floured work surface and fold to deflate. Roll dough into a rectangle to fit the bottom of the pan. Place dough in pan, lightly oil one piece of plastic wrap, and loosely cover dough, oil side in. Allow dough to double in volume.

6. Using your fingertips, make small indents over the entire top of dough. Sprinkle dough with kosher salt and rosemary and then remaining 1 tablespoon extra-virgin olive oil.

Tips, Please

Feel free to use different herbs or spices on top. This is a recipe that begs for experimentation.

7. Bake on a 17¼×11½×1-inch baking pan at 350°F for 25 minutes or until golden brown. Remove bread from the pan and place on wire rack to cool. Cut into 8 pieces.

Oatmeal Pizza Dough

Oatmeal works well with sweet and savory toppings. Try this dough when your sweet tooth calls. Or when it's really talking to you, try the Sweet Oatmeal Pizza Dough variation.

$\frac{1}{2}$ cup rolled oats (not instant)

$1\frac{3}{8}$ cups 105°F to 110°F water

$2\frac{1}{4}$ tsp. dried instant yeast (1 packet)

2 TB. honey

3 or 4 cups bread flour

$1\frac{1}{2}$ tsp. salt

1 tsp. vegetable oil

Yield: 2 (10-inch) pizzas

Prep time:
3 hours

Serving size:
$\frac{1}{3}$ pizza

1. In a small bowl, soak oats in $\frac{3}{4}$ cup water for 1 hour.

2. After oats have soaked, and in another bowl, add yeast to remaining water and stir until dissolved. Add honey and mix again.

3. In a large bowl, combine 3 cups bread flour and salt, and mix thoroughly with a wooden spoon. Add water and yeast mixture to the bowl and mix. Add oats and water combination and mix, adding additional flour 2 tablespoons at a time as necessary so dough holds together and you can knead it but it still remains very soft and sticky.

4. Sprinkle some flour on your work surface, place dough on the surface, and knead dough for 8 minutes.

5. Add oil to the empty bowl, and swirl the bowl to coat the inside. Don't worry if there's a little oil left in the bottom of the bowl. Return dough to the bowl, and turn dough to coat with oil. Cover bowl with plastic wrap, and let dough double in volume.

6. When dough has doubled in volume, turn out onto a floured work surface and fold to deflate. Divide dough into two parts, and form each into a ball. Lightly oil two pieces of plastic wrap, each large enough to cover one ball, and loosely cover each ball, oil side in. Allow to double in volume.

7. Gently deflate balls, and form each into a 10-inch pizza. Add toppings and bake according to the recipe directions.

Variation: For **Sweet Oatmeal Pizza Dough,** reduce water to 1¼ cups and increase honey to ½ cup.

 Tips, Please

You can also try soaking ½ cup raisins in 1 cup hot water ahead of time, draining them, and adding them to the dough with the water and yeast mixture in step 3.

Mixed-Grain Pizza Dough

This dough boasts a complex and pleasant flavor without being on the gravely side of earthy crunchy.

¼ cup rolled oats (not instant)

¼ cup wheat bran

¼ cup yellow cornmeal

¼ cup rye flour

¼ cup buckwheat flour

1½ cups 105°F to 110°F water

1⅛ tsp. dried instant yeast (½ packet)

3 or 4 cups bread flour

1½ tsp. salt

1 tsp. vegetable oil

Yield: 2 (10-inch) pizzas
Prep time:
4 hours
Serving size:
⅓ pizza

1. In a medium bowl, mix oats, wheat bran, cornmeal, rye flour, and buckwheat flour. Add 1 cup water and soak for 1 hour.

2. After oats have soaked, and in another small bowl, add yeast to remaining water, and stir until dissolved.

3. In a large bowl, combine 3 cups bread flour and salt, and mix thoroughly with a wooden spoon. Add water and grain combination and mix. Add water and yeast mixture and mix, adding bread flour 2 tablespoons at a time until dough starts to come away from the sides of the bowl but there are still some strands sticking.

4. Sprinkle some flour on your work surface, place dough on the surface, and knead dough for 10 minutes.

5. Add oil to the empty bowl, and swirl the bowl to coat the inside. Don't worry if there's a little oil left in the bottom of the bowl. Return dough to the bowl, and turn dough to coat with oil. Cover the bowl with plastic wrap, and let dough double in volume.

6. When dough has doubled in volume, turn out onto a floured work surface and fold to deflate. Divide dough into two parts, and form each into a ball. Lightly oil two pieces of plastic wrap, each large enough to cover one ball, and loosely cover each ball, oil side in. Allow to double in volume.

Tips, Please

When working with a sticky dough, lightly coat your hands with vegetable oil to keep the dough from sticking to you as you handle it.

7. Gently deflate balls, and form each into a 10-inch pizza. Add toppings and bake according to the recipe directions.

Naan Dough

These flatbreads are great on their own or as the base for a topping. Just split them, add a filling, and put them in your panini grill.

1⅛ tsp. dried instant yeast (½ packet)

¾ cups 105°F to 110°F water

2 TB. butter

3 or 4 cups bread flour

1½ tsp. salt

⅔ cup plain yogurt

1 tsp. vegetable oil

Yield: 12 loaves
Prep time:
3 hours
Cook time:
2 minutes
Serving size:
2 loaves

1. In a small bowl, add yeast to water, and stir until dissolved.

2. In a small saucepan over high heat, clarify butter by heating until melted, solids separate out, and any water boils out.

3. In a large bowl, combine 3 cups flour and salt, and mix with a wooden spoon. Add water and yeast mixture, yogurt, and 1½ tablespoons clarified butter. Add additional flour, ¼ cup at a time as necessary, until dough comes away from the sides of the bowl.

4. Sprinkle some flour on your work surface, place dough on the surface, and knead dough for 10 minutes.

5. Add vegetable oil to the empty bowl, and swirl the bowl to coat the inside. Don't worry if there's a little oil left in the bottom of the bowl. Return dough to the bowl, and turn dough to coat with oil. Cover bowl with plastic wrap, and let dough double in volume.

6. When dough has doubled in volume, turn out onto a floured work surface and fold to deflate. Divide dough into 12 pieces. Flatten each piece of dough into an oval about 6 inches long.

7. Heat a pizza stone or unglazed tiles in 500°F oven.

8. Carefully put 1 piece of dough onto your palm, reach into the oven, flip dough onto the stone, and repeat so each stone holds 2 breads.

Cook 1 minute or until you see brown spots on the bottom when you lift up an edge with a spatula or tongs. Turn breads over, and cook until that side also has brown spots.

9. As breads are done, brush one side of each with melted butter, stack, and keep wrapped inside a cloth towel.

Secret Ingredient

Another way to clarify butter is to put it into a microwaveable container (like a 2-cup measuring cup) and microwave it for 90 seconds or until the butter is melted, the solids separate out, and any water boils off.

White Sour Starter

Forget a packaged starter. You can create your own tangy sourdough doughs. It requires a little patience and work on your part, but the results are worth it.

Starter:

⅛ tsp. dried instant yeast

1 cup hot 105°F to 110°F water

¾ cup all-purpose flour

First feeding:

1½ cups all-purpose flour

1 cup lukewarm water

Second feeding:

1½ cups all-purpose flour

½ cup water

Third feeding:

1½ cups all-purpose flour

½ cup water

Yield: 5 cups starter
Prep time:
2 days

1. To make starter, dissolve yeast in water. Put ¾ cup flour in a bowl, and whisk in water and yeast mixture. Cover the bowl with plastic wrap, and leave at room temperature for approximately 24 hours or until you see bubbles on the top and it smells slightly sour.

2. For first feeding, stir down starter. Add 1¼ cups all-purpose flour and water to the bowl and whisk together. Sprinkle remaining ¼ cup flour over surface, cover with plastic, and let sit for about 6 to 8 hours or until wide cracks form in the top flour covering.

3. For the second feeding, stir down what you have. Whisk in 1¼ cups flour and ½ cup water. Sprinkle remaining ¼ cup flour over the surface, cover with plastic, and let sit for about 6 to 8 hours or until wide cracks form in the top flour covering.

4. For the third feeding, stir down what you have. Whisk in 1¼ cups flour and ½ cup water. Sprinkle remaining ¼ cup flour on the surface, cover with plastic, and let sit until wide cracks form in the top

flour covering. Use whatever amount you need for sourdough pizza or bread dough recipe, and store leftovers as described earlier in this chapter.

Secret Ingredient

Fake sourdough is made with vinegar. The real stuff ferments over a few days, offering a natural tang that can't be mistaken. If you feel adventurous, omit the yeast in the starter and see if wild yeast will do the trick. Give the starter up to 72 hours; if it isn't bubbling, toss it out and start over. Using wild yeast is less predictable, but the flavor is even better.

Rye Sour Starter

Many people don't realize that the tang of great rye bread products comes from rye sour. Again, you'll have to put in a little work, but you'll be well rewarded.

Starter:

⅛ tsp. dried instant yeast

1 cup 105°F to 110°F water

¾ cup rye flour

1 tsp. ground caraway seed

First feeding:

1½ cups all-purpose flour

1 cup lukewarm water

Second feeding:

1½ cups all-purpose flour

½ cup water

Third feeding:

1½ cups all-purpose flour

½ cup water

Yield: 5 cups starter

Prep time:
2 days

1. To make starter, dissolve yeast in water in a bowl. Mix in flour and caraway seed. Cover bowl with plastic wrap, and leave at room temperature for approximately 24 hours or until you see bubbles on the top and it smells slightly sour.

2. For first feeding, stir down starter. Add 1¼ cups all-purpose flour and water to bowl, and whisk together. Sprinkle remaining ¼ cup flour over surface, cover with plastic, and let sit for about 6 to 8 hours, or until wide cracks form in the top flour covering.

3. For the second feeding, stir down what you have. Whisk in 1¼ cups flour and ½ cup water. Sprinkle remaining ¼ cup flour over the surface, cover with plastic, and let sit for about 6 to 8 hours, or until wide cracks form in the top flour covering.

4. For the third feeding, stir down what you have. Whisk in 1¼ cups flour and ½ cup water. Sprinkle remaining ¼ cup flour on the surface, cover with plastic, and let sit until wide cracks form in the top flour covering. Use whatever amount you need for sourdough pizza or bread dough recipe, and store leftovers as I describe earlier in this chapter.

Secret Ingredient

The principles of rye sour are the same as white, and you can use the same tips to store, replenish, and increase it.

Sourdough Pizza Dough

Sometimes nothing will hit the spot like the tang of sourdough bread.

1⅛ tsp. dried instant yeast (½ packet)

1 cup 105°F to 110°F water

1¾ to 2¼ cups bread flour

2 cups cake flour

2 tsp. salt

1 cup White Sour Starter (recipe earlier in this chapter)

1 tsp. vegetable oil

Yield: 2 (12-inch) pizzas
Prep time:
2 hours
Serving size:
⅓ pizza

1. In a small bowl, add yeast to water and stir until dissolved.

2. In a large bowl, combine 1¾ cups bread flour, cake flour, and salt, and mix thoroughly with a wooden spoon. Add water and yeast mixture and White Sour Starter to the bowl, and mix until all ingredients are combined and strands of dough still cling to the sides of the bowl.

3. Sprinkle bread flour on your work surface, place dough on surface, and knead dough for 10 minutes. Add additional bread flour, 2 table-spoons at a time, as necessary so dough holds together but is still extremely soft.

4. Add oil to the empty bowl, and swirl the bowl to coat the inside. Don't worry if there's a little oil left in the bottom of the bowl. Return dough to the bowl, and turn dough to coat with oil. Cover bowl with plastic wrap, and let dough double in volume.

5. When dough has doubled in volume, turn out onto a floured work surface and fold dough to deflate. Divide dough into two parts, and form each into a ball. Lightly oil two pieces of plastic wrap, each large enough to cover one ball, and loosely cover each ball, oil side in. Allow dough to double in volume.

6. Gently deflate balls, and form each into a 12-inch pizza. Add toppings and bake according to the recipe directions.

Hot Stuff

When you're baking sourdough, be sure you start a few days ahead of time to make the sour if you don't have any ready.

Sourdough Rye Pizza Dough

The rye sour taste is like putting a deli inside your pizza oven.

1⅛ tsp. dried instant yeast (½ packet)

1 cup 105°F to 110°F water

2 to 3 cups bread flour

1 cup rye flour

1½ tsp. salt

1 tsp. ground caraway seed (optional)

1 tsp. whole caraway seed (optional)

1 cup Rye Sour Starter (recipe earlier in this chapter)

1 tsp. vegetable oil

Yield: 2 (12-inch) pizzas
Prep time: 2 hours
Serving size: ⅓ pizza

1. In a small bowl, add yeast to water and stir until dissolved.

2. In a large bowl, combine 2 cups bread flour, rye flour, salt, ground caraway seed (if using), and whole caraway seed (if using), and mix thoroughly with a wooden spoon. Add water and yeast mixture and Rye Sour Starter to the bowl, and mix until all ingredients are combined and strands of dough still cling to the sides of the bowl.

3. Sprinkle flour on your work surface, place dough on surface, and knead dough for 10 minutes. Add additional bread flour, 2 tablespoons at a time, as necessary so dough holds together but is still extremely soft.

4. Add oil to the empty bowl, and swirl the bowl to coat the inside. Don't worry if there's a little oil left in the bottom of the bowl. Return dough to the bowl, and turn dough to coat with oil. Cover bowl with plastic wrap, and let dough double in volume.

5. When dough has doubled in volume, turn out onto a floured work surface and fold dough to deflate. Divide dough into two parts, and

form each into a ball. Lightly oil two pieces of plastic wrap, each large enough to cover one ball, and loosely cover each ball, oil side in. Allow to double in volume.

6. Gently deflate balls, and form each into a 12-inch pizza. Add toppings and bake according to the recipe directions.

Secret Ingredient _____

You don't *have* to add the whole caraway, but combined with the sourdough, it's a nice touch.

4

Just *Loaf*-ing: Bread Doughs

In This Chapter

◆ Whole- and mixed-grain breads

◆ Sour dough loaves

◆ Real Italian breads

Using the same basic techniques you used in making pizza dough, you now bake some fresh bread for panini. And as with the pizza doughs, in this chapter, I offer a variety of dough choices for the range of sandwiches you'll be making.

Many of the doughs here, though not all, use oil and sugar. And like with the pizza dough, if you've got too much, you can store the extra in the freezer. Be warned though: others may tear through the hot fresh bread faster than you can imagine.

Note: All the prep times listed for the following recipes include the rise time.

Rye Bread

Rye bread is an easy way to add some excitement to a sandwich.

2¼ cups 105°F to 110°F water

2 cups rye flour

2¼ tsp. dried instant yeast (1 packet)

4 or 5 cups bread flour

2 tsp. ground caraway seed (optional)

2 TB. whole caraway seeds (optional)

1 TB. salt

1 tsp. vegetable oil

Yield: 2 loaves
Prep time: 3 hours
Cook time: 25 minutes
Serving size: 2 slices

1. In a small bowl, add 1 cup water to rye flour. Let soak for 20 minutes.

2. In another bowl, add yeast to remaining water, and stir until dissolved.

3. In a large bowl, combine 4 cups bread flour, rye flour, ground caraway seed (if using), 1 tablespoon whole caraway seed (if using), and salt, and mix thoroughly with a wooden spoon. Add water and yeast mixture and rye flour and water mixture to the bowl, and mix. Add additional bread flour, 2 tablespoons at a time as necessary, until dough comes away from the sides of the bowl.

4. Sprinkle flour on work surface, place dough on surface, and knead dough for 10 minutes until dough is satiny.

5. Add vegetable oil to the empty bowl, and swirl the bowl to coat the inside. Don't worry if there's a little oil left in the bottom of the bowl. Return dough to the bowl, and turn dough to coat with oil. Cover the bowl with plastic wrap, and let dough double in volume.

6. When dough has doubled in volume, turn out onto a floured work surface and fold to deflate. Divide dough into 2 parts. Shape each portion of dough into a loaf, and place in 2 greased 8½-inch loaf pans. Lightly oil two pieces of plastic wrap, each large enough to cover one pan, and loosely cover each pan, oil side in. Allow top of bread to reach top of pan.

7. Preheat the oven to 350°F. Remove the plastic from the pans, and brush each loaf with water. Sprinkle tops with remaining 1 tablespoon caraway seeds (if using). Bake 25 minutes or until top is golden brown and bottom, when removed from the pan, sounds hollow when tapped.

White Bread

This is a classic white sandwich bread.

2¼ tsp. dried instant yeast (1 packet)

2¼ cups 105°F to 110°F water

6 or 7 cups all-purpose flour

¼ cup low-fat powdered milk

1 TB. sugar

1½ tsp. salt

3 TB. melted butter

1 tsp. vegetable oil

Yield: 2 loaves
Prep time: 3 hours
Cook time: 25 minutes
Serving size: 2 slices

1. In a small bowl, add yeast to water, and stir until dissolved.

2. In a large bowl, combine 5 cups flour, powdered milk, sugar, and salt, and mix thoroughly.

3. Add 2 tablespoons melted butter to water and yeast mixture, and mix with a wooden spoon, adding additional flour, 2 tablespoons at a time as necessary, so dough comes away from the sides of the bowl.

4. Sprinkle flour on your work surface, place dough on surface, and knead dough for 10 minutes until dough is satiny.

5. Add vegetable oil to the empty bowl, and swirl the bowl to coat the inside. Don't worry if there's a little oil left in the bottom of the bowl. Return dough to the bowl, and turn dough to coat with oil. Cover bowl with plastic wrap, and let dough double in volume.

6. When dough has doubled in volume, turn out onto a floured work surface and fold to deflate. (If you're feeling lazy, you can deflate dough in the bowl as described in Chapter 2.) Divide dough into 2 parts. Shape each portion of dough into a loaf, and place in 2 greased 8½-inch loaf pans. Lightly oil two pieces of plastic wrap, each large enough to cover one pan, and loosely cover each pan, oil side in. Allow top of bread to reach top of pan.

Tips, Please _____

If you don't have powdered milk, combine 1 cup water and 1 cup milk, both at 105°F to 110°F, and dissolve yeast in that.

7. Preheat the oven to 350°F. Remove the plastic from the pans, and brush each loaf with remaining 1 tablespoon melted butter. Bake for 25 minutes or until top is golden brown and bottom, when removed from pan, sounds hollow when tapped.

Variation: For **Sweet White Bread,** replace sugar with ½ cup honey and reduce water to 2 cups.

Whole-Wheat Bread

The whole-wheat flour adds a nutty taste to this hearty dough.

2¼ tsp. dried instant yeast (1 packet)

2¼ cups 105°F to 110°F water

4 or 5 cups bread flour

2 cups whole-wheat flour

2 tsp. salt

3 TB. melted butter

¼ cup honey

1 tsp. vegetable oil

Yield: 2 loaves
Prep time:
3 hours
Cook time:
25 minutes
Serving size:
2 slices

1. In a small bowl, add yeast to water, and stir until dissolved.

2. In a large bowl, combine 3 cups bread flour, 2 cups whole-wheat flour, and salt, and mix thoroughly with a wooden spoon. Add water and yeast mixture, 2 tablespoons melted butter, and honey to the bowl, and mix. Add additional bread flour, 2 tablespoons at a time as necessary, so dough comes away from the sides of the bowl.

3. Sprinkle flour on your work surface, place dough on surface, and knead dough for 10 minutes until dough is satiny.

4. Add vegetable oil to the empty bowl, and swirl the bowl to coat the inside. Don't worry if there's a little oil left in the bottom of the bowl. Return dough to the bowl, and turn dough to coat with oil. Cover the bowl with plastic wrap, and let dough double in volume.

5. When dough has doubled in volume, turn out onto a floured work surface and fold to deflate. Divide dough into 2 parts. Shape each portion of dough into a loaf, and place in 2 greased 8½-inch loaf pans. Lightly oil two pieces of plastic wrap, each large enough to cover one pan, and loosely cover each pan, oil side in. Allow top of bread to reach top of pan.

6. Preheat the oven to 350°F. Remove the plastic from the pans, and brush each loaf with remaining 1 tablespoon melted butter. Bake 25 minutes or until top is golden brown and bottom, when removed from the pan, sounds hollow when tapped.

Variation: For **Buckwheat Bread,** replace whole-wheat flour with buckwheat flour.

Secret Ingredient

Most whole-wheat doughs use some white flour to lighten the texture, and this is no different. But this recipe has a high percentage of whole wheat and adds honey as the sweetener for a stronger flavor.

Oatmeal Bread

The rolled oats add flavor and an interesting texture to this dough.

1 cup rolled oats (not instant)

2¾ cups 105°F to 110°F water

2¼ tsp. dried instant yeast (1 packet)

5 or 6 cups all-purpose flour

1 TB. salt

¼ cup honey

1 tsp. vegetable oil

Yield: 2 loaves
Prep time:
3 hours
Cook time:
25 minutes
Serving size:
2 slices

1. In a small bowl, add oats to 1 cup water and soak for 15 minutes.

2. In another small bowl, add yeast to remaining water, and stir until dissolved.

3. In a large bowl, combine 4 cups flour, rolled oats, and salt, and mix thoroughly with a wooden spoon. Add water and yeast mixture, honey, and oats and water mixture. Mix. Add additional flour, 2 tablespoons at a time as necessary, until dough comes away from the sides of the bowl.

4. Sprinkle flour on your work surface, place dough on surface, and knead dough for 10 minutes until dough is satiny.

5. Add vegetable oil to the empty bowl, and swirl the bowl to coat the inside. Don't worry if there's a little oil left in the bottom of the bowl. Return dough to the bowl, and turn dough to coat with oil. Cover the bowl with plastic wrap, and let dough double in volume.

6. When dough has doubled in volume, turn out onto a floured work surface and fold to deflate. Divide dough into 2 parts. Shape each portion of dough into a loaf, and place in 2 greased 8½-inch loaf pans. Lightly oil two pieces of plastic wrap, each large enough to cover one pan, and loosely cover each pan, oil side in. Allow top of bread to reach top of pan.

Tips, Please _____

Soaking the oats before making the dough helps keep the bread moist.

7. Preheat the oven to 350°F. Remove the plastic from the pans, and brush each loaf with water. Bake 25 minutes or until top is medium brown and bottom, when removed from pan, sounds hollow when tapped.

Variation: For **Sweet Oatmeal Bread,** reduce water to 2 cups and increase honey to ¾ cups.

Sourdough Bread

This recipe has an open crumb and tangy flavor for adding zip to panini.

4½ tsp. dried instant yeast (2 packets; do not increase)

2 cups 105°F to 110°F water

¼ cup honey

1 cup White Sour Starter (recipe in Chapter 3)

5 or 6 cups bread flour

1 TB. salt

1 tsp. vegetable oil

Yield: **2 loaves**
Prep time:
3 hours
Cook time:
25 minutes
Serving size:
2 slices

1. In a medium bowl, add yeast to water, and stir until dissolved. Add honey and mix with wooden spoon. Mix in sour starter.

2. In a large bowl, combine 5 cups flour and salt, and mix thoroughly with a wooden spoon. Add yeast mixture, and mix. Add additional flour, ¼ cup at a time as necessary; strands of dough should still cling to side of bowl.

3. Sprinkle flour on your work surface, place dough on surface, and knead dough for 5 minutes until dough is smooth.

4. Add vegetable oil to the empty bowl, and swirl the bowl to coat the inside. Don't worry if there's a little oil left in the bottom of the bowl. Return dough to the bowl, and turn dough to coat with oil. Cover bowl with plastic wrap, and let dough rise 30 minutes.

5. Turn dough out onto a lightly oiled work surface, and fold to deflate. Return to bowl and recover with plastic.

6. When dough has doubled in volume, turn out onto a floured work surface and fold to deflate. Divide dough into 2 parts. Shape each portion of dough into an oval loaf and place onto a heavily floured surface. Cover with lightly oiled plastic wrap, and allow dough to double in size.

7. Place a pizza stone or tiles into the oven and preheat to 425°F. Remove plastic from dough, carefully place loaves onto a cornmeal-covered peel, and slide them onto the stone or tiles. Bake 25 minutes or until top is golden brown and bottom, when removed from pan, sounds hollow when tapped.

Tips, Please

If you want a sandwich loaf, use 2 greased 8½-inch loaf pans, and shape the dough accordingly.

Sourdough Rye Bread

For the true deli panino, this is the bread to use.

4½ tsp. dried instant yeast (2 packets; do not increase)

2 cups 105°F to 110°F water

¼ cup honey

3½ to 4½ cups bread flour

3 cups rye flour

1 TB. salt

2 tsp. ground caraway seed (optional)

1 TB. whole caraway seed (optional)

1 cup Rye Sour Starter (recipe in Chapter 3)

1 tsp. vegetable oil

Yield: 2 loaves
Prep time:
3 hours
Cook time:
25 minutes
Serving size:
2 slices

1. In a small bowl, add yeast to water, and stir until dissolved. Add honey.

2. In a large bowl, combine 3½ cups bread flour, rye flour, salt, ground caraway seeds (if using), and whole caraway seeds (if using), and mix thoroughly with a wooden spoon. Add yeast mixture, Rye Sour Starter, and mix. Add additional flour, 2 tablespoons at a time as necessary; strands of dough should still cling to side of bowl.

3. Sprinkle flour on your work surface, place dough on surface, and knead dough for 5 minutes until dough is smooth.

4. Add vegetable oil to the empty bowl, and swirl the bowl to coat the inside. Don't worry if there's a little oil left in the bottom of the bowl. Return dough to the bowl, and turn dough to coat with oil. Cover the bowl with plastic wrap, and let dough rise 30 minutes.

5. Turn dough out onto a lightly oiled work surface, and fold to deflate. Return dough to the bowl, and recover with plastic.

6. When dough has doubled in volume, turn out onto a floured work surface and fold to deflate. Divide dough into 2 parts. Shape each portion of dough into an oval loaf, and place onto heavily floured surface. Cover with lightly oiled plastic wrap, and allow dough to double in size.

7. Place a pizza stone or tiles into the oven and preheat to 425°F. Remove plastic from dough, carefully place loaves onto a cornmeal-covered peel, and slide then onto the stone or tiles. Bake 25 minutes or until top is golden brown and bottom, when removed from pan, sounds hollow when tapped.

Secret Ingredient

The longer you've been developing your sour, the better the bread's flavor will be.

Ciabatta

This is a classic rustic bread with large holes inside and big taste throughout.

2¼ tsp. dried instant yeast (1 packet)

2½ cups 105°F to 110°F water

6 or 7 cups all-purpose flour

1 TB. salt

1 tsp. olive oil

2 cups boiling water

Yield: 2 loaves or 10 rolls
Prep time: 3 hours
Cook time: 25 minutes
Serving size: 2 slices or 1 roll

1. In a small bowl, add 1⅛ teaspoon yeast to 2 cups water and stir until dissolved.

2. In a large bowl, add 3 cups flour. Add water and yeast mixture, and whisk until blended. Cover the bowl with plastic wrap, and let biga expand in volume until it stops—about triple in volume and when deep wrinkles appear on the surface. Stir down biga before the center sinks.

3. In a small bowl, add 1⅛ teaspoon yeast to ½ cup water and stir until dissolved. Add yeast mixture to biga, and mix thoroughly.

4. In a large bowl, mix salt and 3 cups flour. Add to biga, and mix thoroughly. Dough will be very sticky, and strands will cling to the side of the bowl.

5. Heavily flour your work surface, and turn dough out onto surface, scraping the bowl clean of dough. Knead dough for 5 minutes. Let dough rest for 10 minutes and then knead another 5 minutes.

6. Add oil to the empty bowl, and swirl the bowl to coat the inside. Don't worry if there's a little oil left in the bottom of the bowl. Return dough to the bowl, turn dough to coat with oil. Cover the bowl with plastic wrap, and let dough rise until puffy, about 30 to 45 minutes.

7. Turn dough out onto heavily floured work surface, and fold dough to release gasses. Brush excess flour from dough and return dough to the bowl. Recover bowl with plastic wrap and allow dough to rise until almost doubled in size.

8. Turn dough out onto a heavily floured work surface, being careful not to deflate it. Gently push dough into a rectangular shape and cut into two long rectangular loaves. Using a dough scraper, gently move one loaf so a few inches of space separates the two loaves. Let dough rise another 30 to 45 minutes or until it has regained any volume it lost.

9. Place a pizza stone or tiles onto the middle oven rack and put a roasting pan on the oven floor. Preheat the oven to 450°F. Heavily cover a peel with cornmeal. Pour boiling water into the roasting pan, and close the oven for 5 minutes.

Secret Ingredient

This Italian bread is probably the trickiest dough in the book because you have to handle the risen dough without deflating it. Instead of making 2 long loaves, you can cut the dough into 10 equal-size rectangular rolls. Or make 2 round loaves by forming balls instead of rectangles.

10. Carefully place one loaf on the peel so the side that was in the flour is now facing up. Slide the loaf into oven and close the door. Recover peel with cornmeal, and repeat with the second loaf. Bake about 25 minutes or until top is medium to dark brown and bottom, when removed from pan, sounds hollow when tapped.

Mixed-Grain Bread

The complex taste of this bread might make you forget that the mix of grains is good for you, too.

½ cup rolled oats (not instant)

¼ cup wheat bran

¼ cup yellow cornmeal

¼ cup buckwheat flour

¼ cup rye flour

2½ cups 105°F to 110°F water

4½ tsp. dried instant yeast (2 packets; do not increase)

2 eggs

3½ to 4 cups bread flour

1 TB. salt

¼ cup sugar

1 tsp. vegetable oil

Yield: 2 loaves
Prep time: 3½ hours
Cook time: 25 minutes
Serving size: 2 slices

1. In a medium bowl, combine oats, wheat bran, cornmeal, buckwheat flour, and rye flour. Add 1 cup water, and let soak for 20 minutes.

2. In a small bowl, add yeast to 1½ cups water, and stir until dissolved. Beat eggs, and add to yeast mixture.

3. In a large bowl, combine 3½ cups bread flour, salt, and sugar, and mix thoroughly with a wooden spoon. Add yeast mixture and mix. Add water and grains from step 1, and mix. Add additional bread flour, 2 tablespoons at a time as necessary, until dough just comes away from the sides of the bowl but is still slightly sticky.

4. Sprinkle flour on your work surface, place dough on surface, and knead dough for 10 minutes or until dough surface is smooth but remains slightly tacky.

5. Add vegetable oil to the empty bowl, and swirl the bowl to coat the inside. Don't worry if there's a little oil left in the bottom of the bowl. Return dough to the bowl, and turn dough to coat with oil. Cover bowl with plastic wrap. Let dough double in volume.

6. When dough has doubled in volume, turn out onto a floured work surface and fold to deflate. Divide dough into 2 parts. Shape each portion of dough into a loaf, and place in 2 greased 8½-inch loaf pans. Lightly oil two pieces of plastic wrap, each large enough to cover one pan, and loosely cover each pan, oil side in. Allow top of bread to reach top of pan.

7. Preheat the oven to 375°F. Remove the plastic from the pans, and brush each loaf with water. Sprinkle tops with remaining caraway seeds (if using). Bake 25 minutes or until top is golden brown and bottom, when removed from pan, sounds hollow when tapped.

Chapter 5

It's the Tops: Toppings

In This Chapter

- ◆ Great-tasting sauces for your pizzas and panini
- ◆ Quick tomato sauces
- ◆ Tips for storing extra sauce

Sauces, relishes, condiments, and accoutrements can make the difference between two dishes that otherwise share the same ingredients. Think of them as the options that tailor your meal to your preferences.

You can make most of these sauces a day ahead to make the pizza assembly go faster. Store them in the refrigerator. The only exception is the white sauce and its variations, because I've never found it to keep particularly well. Luckily, a white sauce only takes about 15 minutes to prepare. I've never frozen most of these sauces other than the Pomodoro Fresca sauce. If you want to keep some handy (it's also good on pasta), line an ice cube tray with plastic wrap, pushing the wrap down into the depressions. Fill the depressions with sauce and put the tray in the freezer. When it sets, you can remove the cubes and store them in a container in the freezer. When you want some, take out just enough cubes to satisfy your needs.

Pomodoro Fresca Sauce

This light tomato sauce goes together quickly and is terrific on pasta and pizza alike.

1½ TB. olive oil

1 small onion, chopped

2 cloves garlic, minced

1 (28-oz.) can imported Italian plum tomatoes, drained

1 tsp. salt

¼ cup red wine

¼ cup chopped fresh basil or 2 TB. dried

Yield: 2 cups
Prep time:
15 minutes
Cook time:
10 minutes
Serving size:
⅓ cup for 10-inch pizza or 1 or 2 tablespoons for a panino

1. Heat oil in a medium frying pan over medium-high heat. Add onion and cook, stirring occasionally, until translucent. Add garlic and cook, stirring occasionally, until garlic is soft.

2. Add tomatoes, breaking them up into ¼-inch pieces. Add salt and wine, and cook, stirring occasionally, until no watery liquid remains and sauce is thick.

3. Add basil and cook another minute.

Variation: For **Spicy Tomato Sauce,** add ½ teaspoon red pepper flakes with the salt.

Secret Ingredient

If you're used to American pizza, this chunky sauce might seem unusual, but in Italy, pizzaioli typically put crushed tomatoes on their pies. The intense oven heat eliminates the water and caramelizes some of the sugars, sweetening the result—for those of you who don't have a wood-fired oven.

Salsa

This is my wife's recipe and a favorite of our family and guests. If you're not crazy about cilantro, substitute parsley sprigs for any or all of the cilantro.

1 (28-oz.) can imported diced tomatoes, drained with liquid reserved

1 large onion, diced

1 small green bell pepper, diced

2 cloves garlic, minced

10 sprigs cilantro, minced

2 TB. fresh lime juice, or 2 TB. red wine vinegar

2 jalapeño peppers, stems removed and chopped

Salt

Yield: 2 cups
Prep time: 25 minutes
Serving size: ⅓ cup for 10-inch pizza or 1 or 2 tablespoons for a panino

1. In a medium bowl, mix drained tomatoes, onion, pepper, garlic, cilantro, lime juice, and jalapeños. Season with salt.

2. Allow salsa to sit in the refrigerator for at least 2 hours to let the flavors blend.

Hot Stuff

Take care handling jalapeño peppers. Wearing disposable plastic gloves or put disposable plastic bags over your hands, cut off stems and then roughly chop the flesh. To reduce the amount of spice, you can split the jalapeños, use the back of a knife to scrape off the seeds, discard the seeds, and chop the peppers. Be sure not to touch your eyes unconsciously while handling the jalapeños.

Cocktail Sauce

When ketchup seems a little boring, the horseradish in this sauce gives your taste buds a kick.

½ cup ketchup

1 tsp. prepared horseradish

¼ tsp. Worcestershire sauce (optional)

⅛ tsp. hot pepper sauce (optional)

Yield: ½ cup
Prep time: 2 minutes
Serving size: ⅓ cup for 10-inch pizza or 1 or 2 tablespoons for a panino

1. In a bowl, mix ketchup, horseradish, Worcestershire sauce (if using), and hot pepper sauce (if using).

Secret Ingredient

Now there's never a reason to go without cocktail sauce. This is also a superior dip for french fries, as I first learned when a waiter many years ago at a storied restaurant name in Boston.

White Sauce

Make an ordinary meal into a creamy satisfying delight with this sauce. (Be sure to check out the variations for more ideas.)

1 cup whole or 2% milk

1½ TB. butter

1½ TB. all-purpose flour

¼ tsp. nutmeg

Salt and white pepper

Yield: 1 cup
Prep time:
20 minutes
Cook time:
10 minutes
Serving size:
⅓ cup for 10-inch pizza or 1 or 2 tablespoons for a panino

1. In a saucepan over medium heat, cook milk until small bubbles form at the edge.

2. In another saucepan over high heat, melt butter. Add flour and cook until froth subsides but before mixture turns brown. Add milk all at once. Whisk until smooth and thickened.

3. Add nutmeg and season with salt and white pepper.

Variations: For **Dill Cream Sauce,** replace nutmeg with 1 teaspoon chopped dill. For **Cheese Sauce,** replace nutmeg with ½ cup grated Parmesan cheese. For **Poultry Cream Sauce,** replace milk with chicken stock. For **Shellfish Cream Sauce,** replace milk with clam juice. For **Greek Egg-Enriched White Sauce,** omit nutmeg but prepare White Sauce as directed. When done, remove from heat. Beat 1 egg in a bowl and very slowly whisk in ½ cup sauce. When thoroughly blended, pour back into pot of sauce. If sauce curdles, pass it through a sieve.

Tips, Please

A sauce has thickened sufficiently if you dip a wooden spoon into the sauce, pull the spoon out, run your finger across the back of the spoon, and a clear path through the sauce remains.

Beef Gravy

A little bit of this gravy can make a pizza or panino into comfort food.

1 cup beef stock

1½ TB. butter

1½ TB. flour

Salt and pepper

Yield: 1 cup
Prep time: 30 minutes
Serving size: ⅓ cup for 10-inch pizza or 1 or 2 tablespoons for a panino

1. In a saucepan over medium heat, warm up beef stock.

2. In another saucepan over high heat, melt butter. Add flour, and cook until froth subsides and mixture turns light nut brown.

3. Add hot beef stock, and whisk until smooth and thickened. Season with salt and pepper.

Variation: For **Mushroom Sauce,** add ¼ cup red wine and 4 ounces white mushrooms, sliced that have been sautéed in 2 tablespoons butter. Simmer until thick enough to coat back of wooden spoon.

Tips, Please

If you have a beef roast, you can use the pan drippings in this recipe in place of the beef stock. Here's how: remove the roast and heat the pan over high heat. Add 1 cup water and stir, scraping up the crusted juices until they dissolve.

Roasted Bell Pepper

Roasted bell pepper means summer grilling for some folks. This indoor version still adds a summery sweetness to your cooking.

1 bell pepper, any color

Yield: 1 pepper
Prep time:
5 minutes
Cook time:
20 minutes
Serving size:
⅓ pepper for 1 pizza

1. Stick pepper's stem onto long cooking fork. Turn the stovetop burner to high heat, and hold pepper close to the heat. Wait for skin near heat to blister and turn black before turning pepper. Continue turning pepper slowly until most all the skin is blackened.

2. Put blackened pepper into a paper bag and leave for 20 minutes. Remove pepper from the bag, and peel away skin. It should come off easily.

3. Pull off stem, split pepper, and, using back of knife, scrape seeds away.

Secret Ingredient

Roasted bell peppers have a subtler taste than their uncooked cousins. They're perfect as toppings for a pizza or panino, when you want a little extra something but nothing too strong.

Caramel Sauce

"Caramel sauce on pizza?" you ask. "You bet," I reply. Try this caramel sauce when your sweet tooth acts up.

3 cups sugar

⅔ cups water

2 cups heavy cream

1 tsp. vanilla extract (optional)

Yield: 4 cups
Prep time: 15 minutes
Cook time: 25 minutes
Serving size: ⅓ cup for 10-inch pizza or 1 or 2 tablespoons for a panino

1. In a medium saucepan over high heat, add sugar and then water. Do not stir while you let sugar totally dissolve. Periodically dip a pastry brush into cold water and brush the inside of the pan. Do not let any crystals form on the sides of the pan.

Tips, Please

I usually always add the "optional" ingredients. In this case, though, I never use the vanilla extract because my family likes the strong caramel flavor. However, if you like vanilla caramel candies, you might want to try it with vanilla extract.

2. When sugar turns dark amber, put a whisk into the pan and carefully and slowly add cream. Mixture will boil furiously and form a mass. Gently move the whisk and everything will eventually dissolve into a smooth liquid. Add vanilla extract (if using) at this point.

3. Let caramel cool some and pour into a container.

Part 3

It's a Flat, Flat, Flat, Flat World

Good things come in flat packages. In Part 3, you get all the recipes for pizzas. I've included chapters on meat as well as meatless pizzas and internationally inspired pies. But that's not all. What about pizza for breakfast? You bet. I included a chapter for that as well. Well, what are you waiting for?

Chapter 6

Meat the Pizza

In This Chapter

- ◆ Meat makes the pizza (so some say)
- ◆ Sausage and pepperoni prep tips
- ◆ Fish and shellfish on pizzas? Why not?
- ◆ There's a reason deep-dish pizza is so popular
- ◆ Transform entrée recipes into pizzas

From pepperoni to prosciutto, to chicken, beef, salmon, and everything else in between, meat, poultry, and fish are old companions of pizzas. However, because a pizza is in the oven for such a short time, meat generally must be cooked in advance before going onto the pizza.

The exception is small or thin pieces of fish or shellfish, as they cook incredibly quickly. You can use cuts of meat you'd normally cook in other ways, buy something precooked, get the goods from your deli counter, or even use leftovers.

Old Favorites: Pepperoni and Sausage

The two most popular meats for pizza are pepperoni and sausage, and they're both easy enough to make:

1. Pick up ¼ pound meat for each 10-inch pizza. (Be sure to cook raw sausage ahead of time.)

2. Cut the pepperoni into slices about ⅛-inch thick.

Tips, Please

When shopping for link sausage, try sweet or hot Italian sausage. They're great choices for topping your pie.

If you get link sausage (sweet or hot Italian are great choices), cook them first and cut into ⅛-inch slices.

If you can get bulk Italian sausage not in a casing, brown ¼ pound in a pan, drain the grease, let the sausage cool, and break it up into ¼- to ½-inch pieces.

3. Then make a Cheese Pizza (recipe in Chapter 7) and put the meat on top of the cheese before you put the pizza into the oven.

If you're feeling adventurous, try a different type of meat, like thin slices of hard Genoa salami, or try one of the less-than-conventional recipes in this chapter.

Barbecue Pizza

The sweetness and tomato base of barbecue sauce make this pizza seem familiar and exotic at the same time.

1 TB. olive oil (if meat is uncooked)

⅓ lb. thinly sliced steak, chicken breast, or pork roast

⅓ cup barbecue sauce (your favorite)

¼ cup coleslaw, well drained (optional)

¼ cup dill pickle slices, well drained (optional)

Yield: 1 pizza
Prep time:
30 minutes
Cook time:
10 minutes
Serving size:
⅓ to ½ pizza

1. Place a pizza stone or tiles in the oven, and preheat the oven to 500°F. Heavily dust a peel with cornmeal.

2. If meat is uncooked, heat a small saucepan over high heat. Add olive oil and meat, and sauté 4 minutes or until meat is just cooked through. Drain and reserve meat. (Can be done 1 day in advance.)

3. Form dough into pizza crust and place on cornmeal-covered peel. Spread sauce over pizza, and arrange meat slices evenly over top.

4. Bake for 10 minutes or until edges are golden brown. Top with coleslaw and/or pickle slices (if using), cut into slices, and serve.

Tips, Please _____

Coleslaw and pickle slices are traditional additions to barbecue sandwiches in many parts of the South. If you're not feeling very "southern," feel free to omit them from your Barbecue Pizza. If you do use them, add them cold and get an interesting contrast in temperature and texture.

Hawaiian Pizza

No matter how strange this sounds, give it a try. The pineapple brings the Hawaiian accent.

$^1\!/_3$ lb. cooked ham steak

$^1\!/_4$ tsp. ground allspice

$^1\!/_8$ tsp. ground cloves

$^1\!/_3$ cup White Sauce (recipe in Chapter 5)

Pizza Dough I, II, or III or Sourdough Pizza Dough for 1 pizza (recipes/variations in Chapter 3)

$^1\!/_3$ cup ricotta cheese

$^1\!/_3$ cup canned pineapple cubes, drained

Yield: 1 pizza
Prep time: 30 minutes
Cook time: 10 minutes
Serving size: $^1\!/_3$ to $^1\!/_2$ pizza

1. Place a pizza stone or tiles in the oven, and preheat the oven to 500°F. Heavily dust a peel with cornmeal.

2. Cut ham into $^1\!/_4$-inch cubes and set aside.

3. In a small bowl, add allspice and cloves to White Sauce and mix.

4. Form dough into pizza crust and place on cornmeal-covered peel. Spread sauce over pizza, and break up cheese and distribute over pizza. Add ham and pineapple.

5. Bake for 10 minutes or until edges are golden brown, cut into slices, and serve.

Variation: For **Hawaiian Sunset Pizza,** omit allspice and cloves and replace White Sauce with $^1\!/_3$ cup Pomodoro Fresca Sauce.

Deep-Dish Pizza

Take a bite of this satisfying pie, and you'll know why it's a Chicago favorite.

Pizza Dough I, II, or III for 2 pizzas (recipes/variations in Chapter 3)

1 TB. olive oil

1 cup Pomodoro Fresca Sauce (recipe in Chapter 5)

1¼ cups grated mozzarella cheese

½ cup thinly sliced onion

½ cup thinly sliced green bell pepper

¼ lb. cooked bulk Italian sausage

Yield: 1 pizza
Prep time:
30 minutes
Cook time:
30 minutes
Serving size:
¼ to ⅙ pizza

1. Preheat the empty oven to 375°F.

2. Using a rolling pin, roll out dough so it stretches 2 inches beyond the dimensions of a 14-inch deep-dish pizza baking pan. Grease the inside of the pan with olive oil. Lift dough into the pan, stretching if necessary so it covers the bottom and the sides.

3. Spread sauce over pizza. Distribute cheese over pizza, followed by onion slices, bell pepper slices, and sausage.

4. Bake for 30 minutes or until edges are golden brown. Using a spatula, remove pizza from the pan, place on a cutting board, cut into pieces, and serve.

Secret Ingredient

Deep-dish pizza was invented in 1943 in Chicago. The crust is thicker than with the usual type, it cooks in a pan, and you'll probably want to eat it with a knife and a fork, as it's harder to handle. Don't sweat what pan to use too much—use something round about 14 inches across and 2 inches high or a rectangular pan 14×10½×2-inch baking pan. Also, feel free to substitute toppings and sauces to your heart's content.

Reuben Pizza

You won't find this in a New York deli, but after trying it, I bet you wish you could.

Rye Pizza Dough for 1 pizza (variation in Chapter 3)

⅓ cup Thousand Island dressing

⅓ lb. cooked sliced corned beef

¼ lb. thinly sliced Swiss cheese

½ cup sauerkraut, drained

Yield: 1 pizza
Prep time:
30 minutes
Cook time:
10 minutes
Serving size:
⅓ to ½ pizza

1.   Place a pizza stone or tiles in the oven and preheat to 500°F. Heavily dust a peel with cornmeal.

Secret Ingredient

This recipe might sound a bit odd at first, but think of it as a grilled Reuben without one of the pieces of bread. I think you'll change your mind after you give it a try.

2.   Form dough into pizza crust and place on cornmeal-covered peel. Spread Thousand Island dressing on pizza, and top with corned beef. Top with Swiss cheese and then sauerkraut.

3.   Bake for 10 minutes or until edges are golden brown. Using a spatula, remove pizza from the oven, cut into slices, and serve.

Salmon and Dill Cream Sauce Pizza

This elegant combination of tastes brings a level of sophistication to pizza's casual style.

Sourdough Pizza Dough for 1 pizza (recipe in Chapter 3)

½ lb. salmon fillet

⅓ cup Dill Cream Sauce (variation in Chapter 5)

⅛ cup drained *capers*

Yield: 1 pizza
Prep time: 30 minutes
Cook time: 8 minutes
Serving size: ⅓ to ½ pizza

1. Place a pizza stone or tiles in the oven and preheat to 500°F. Heavily dust peel with cornmeal.

2. Form dough into pizza crust and place on cornmeal-covered peel. Bake crust for 2 minutes. Remove from the oven with a spatula and replace crust on the peel.

3. Thinly slice salmon. Be sure no bones remain in it.

4. Spread sauce over pizza. Arrange salmon slices over top, and sprinkle capers over all.

5. Bake for 8 minutes or until edges are golden brown and salmon is opaque, cut into slices, and serve.

Doughfinition

Capers aren't youthful hijinks, but rather the flavorful pickled buds of a Mediterranean plant. Get the jarred variety.

Shrimp Pizza

Inspiring this flavor combination was a recipe I saw in the magazine *La Cucina Italiana* for shrimp ravioli with a leek sauce. I left out the leeks here, but you won't miss them.

Whole-Wheat Pizza Dough for 1 pizza (variation in Chapter 3)

⅓ lb. shelled, deveined, uncooked medium shrimp

⅓ cup Shellfish Cream Sauce (variation in Chapter 5)

2 TB. lemon zest

Yield: 1 pizza

Prep time:
30 minutes

Cook time:
8 minutes

Serving size:
⅓ to ½ pizza

1. Place a pizza stone or tiles in the oven and preheat to 500° F. Heavily dust a peel with cornmeal.

2. Form dough into pizza crust and place on cornmeal-covered peel. Bake for 2 minutes, remove from the oven, and replace on the peel.

3. Rinse shrimp, pat dry with paper towels, and scatter over pizza. Spread sauce over pizza. Sprinkle lemon zest on top.

4. Bake for 8 minutes or until edges are golden brown and shrimp is cooked through. Remove pizza from the oven, cut into slices, and serve.

Tips, Please

The shrimp go under the sauce here because they're delicate and this lets them cook through while helping keep them from overcooking. If you want, you can cook the shrimp separately, keeping them warm, and put them on only when the pizza is out of the oven and completely cooked.

Chicken Florentine Pizza

Florentine means a dish with spinach as a major ingredient. This combination of spinach, chicken, onion, and cream sauce will soon become a favorite.

$\frac{1}{3}$ lb. boneless and skinless chicken

$\frac{1}{2}$ small onion

$\frac{1}{4}$ lb. white mushrooms

3 TB. olive oil

Salt and pepper

1 clove garlic, chopped

$\frac{1}{2}$ cup grated Parmesan cheese

Mixed-Grain Pizza Dough for 1 pizza (recipe in Chapter 3)

$\frac{1}{2}$ cup Poultry Cream Sauce (variation in Chapter 5)

$\frac{1}{2}$ (10-oz.) pkg. frozen chopped spinach, thawed

Yield: 1 pizza
Prep time:
30 minutes
Cook time:
10 minutes
Serving size:
$\frac{1}{3}$ to $\frac{1}{2}$ pizza

1. Place a pizza stone or tiles in the oven and preheat to 500°F. Heavily dust a peel with cornmeal.

2. Slice chicken into $\frac{1}{4}$-inch-thick strips and set aside.

3. Cut onion through root end and place the flat side of $\frac{1}{2}$ onion onto a cutting board. Make horizontal cuts $\frac{1}{4}$-inch thick from nonroot end to root. Make vertical cuts $\frac{1}{4}$-inch thick from nonroot end to root. Trim off root, leaving $\frac{1}{4}$-inch thick strips. Set onion aside.

4. Trim mushroom caps and cut mushrooms into approximately $\frac{1}{8}$-inch slices. Set aside.

5. Heat a medium pan over high heat and add $1\frac{1}{2}$ tablespoons olive oil. Add chicken strips and sauté until they just turn opaque. Season with salt and pepper, and remove chicken from the pan.

6. Return the pan to heat and add remaining $1\frac{1}{2}$ tablespoon olive oil. Add onion and cook, stirring occasionally, until it turns translucent. Add garlic and cook, stirring occasionally, until garlic turns translucent. Season with salt and pepper. Remove onions and garlic from the pan.

7. Return the pan to heat and add mushrooms. Cook until soft. Reduce heat to medium, and add Poultry Cream Sauce. Heat through and add cheese, stirring until melted.

8. Form dough into pizza crust and place on cornmeal-covered peel. Bake for 2 minutes or until crust is firm. Remove from the oven.

9. Sprinkle onion and garlic mixture over pizza and then spread sauce over. Scatter spinach on top, and distribute chicken over all.

10. Bake for 10 minutes or until edges are golden brown. Remove pizza from the oven, cut into slices, and serve.

Secret Ingredient

This is an example of adapting a popular dish into a pizza topping. Try your own experiments and creations.

Jambalaya Chicken Pizza

Jambalaya is one of the great culinary inventions of this country. It only seems fitting that it should be on top of a pizza.

Sourdough Pizza Dough for 2 pizzas (recipe in Chapter 3)

3 TB. olive oil

1 small onion, diced

1 rib celery, diced

2 cloves garlic, minced

½ lb. boneless skinless chicken, diced

½ lb. smoked ham, diced

½ lb. andouille sausage or chorizo, diced

1½ cups Spicy Tomato Sauce (variation in Chapter 5)

1 cup shredded mozzarella cheese

Yield: 1 pizza
Prep time: 40 minutes
Cook time: 30 minutes
Serving size: ¼ to ⅙ pizza

1. Preheat the empty oven to 375°F.

2. Using a rolling pin, roll out dough so it stretches 2 inches beyond the dimensions of a 14×2-inch round or 14×10½×2-inch rectangular baking pan. Grease the inside of the pan with 1 tablespoon olive oil. Lift dough into the pan, stretching if necessary so it covers the bottom and the sides.

3. Heat a medium skillet over high heat and add 1 tablespoon olive oil. Add onion and celery and cook, stirring occasionally, until translucent. Add garlic and cook, stirring occasionally, until it turns translucent. Remove all from the pan and reserve.

4. Return the pan to heat and add remaining 1 tablespoon olive oil. Add chicken, ham, and sausage, and cook, stirring occasionally, until chicken just turns opaque. Remove from heat and add onion, celery, and garlic mixture.

5. Spread meat and vegetable mixture over pizza. Spread sauce over top, and sprinkle with cheese.

6. Bake for 30 minutes or until edges are golden brown. Remove pizza from the oven, cut into slices, and serve.

Secret Ingredient

Jambalaya is far less prescriptive than this recipe might have you think. In that spirit, pick and choose which meats to add or substitute at your whim. This is a great dish for whatever you have on hand.

Chapter 7

Garden Variety Pies

In This Chapter

- ◆ Recipes for classic Neapolitan-style pizzas
- ◆ No-sauce pizza? Yes!
- ◆ Indian flatbread pizza—try it, you'll like it

If you're a vegetarian or just looking for a lighter meal, I have just the thing for you: pizza. Nothing says you have to pile the meat on your pie. By adding vegetables, herbs, cheese, and sauce (or not), you can create dishes that will have even the devoted carnivores coming back for more.

On meatless pizzas, cheese often plays a more prominent taste role because there's no heavy, over-riding taste from the meat. I think better cheese makes for better pizza in general, but that's even more true when the cheese is on its own or paired with more delicate-tasting vegetables. So don't skimp: get good-quality cheese and grate or shred it yourself. The results far surpass the small amount of time it takes.

Cheese Pizza

The classic Neapolitan pizza should have enough cheese for taste but not so much that you lose the quality of the sauce and crust.

Pizza Dough I, II, or III for 1 pizza (recipes/variations in Chapter 3)

⅓ cup Pomodoro Fresca Sauce (recipe in Chapter 5)

½ cup grated mozzarella cheese

Yield: 1 pizza
Prep time: 15 minutes
Cook time: 10 minutes
Serving size: ⅓ to ½ pizza

1. Place a pizza stone or tiles in the oven and preheat to 500°F. Heavily dust a peel with cornmeal.

2. Form dough into pizza crust and place on cornmeal-covered peel. Spread sauce over pizza. Sprinkle cheese on top.

3. Bake for 10 minutes or until edges are golden brown. Remove pizza from the oven, cut into slices, and serve.

Tips, Please

If the cheese browns while it cooks, look for a better-quality mozzarella. Or try this: bake the crust for 2 minutes, take it out, put on the sauce and cheese, and return the pizza to the oven to finish baking.

Variations: For a **Veggie Pizza,** top pizza with ¼ cup broccoli florets, ¼ cup sliced or chopped black olives, and ¼ cup chopped walnuts before baking. When cooked, sprinkle with 1 tablespoon balsamic vinegar. For **Mushroom Pizza,** top pizza with ¼ cup trimmed and sliced portobello mushrooms, ¼ cup trimmed and sliced shiitake mushrooms, and ¼ cup trimmed and sliced oyster mushrooms.

Margherita Pizza

Combining basil, tomatoes, and mozzarella is an old Italian culinary tradition.

4 oz. sliced mozzarella cheese

6 fresh basil leaves

Pizza Dough I, II, or III for 1 pizza (recipes/variations in Chapter 3)

⅓ cup Pomodoro Fresca Sauce (recipe in Chapter 5)

1 TB. extra-virgin olive oil

Yield: 1 pizza
Prep time:
15 minutes
Cook time:
10 minutes
Serving size:
⅓ to ½ pizza

1. Place a pizza stone or tiles in the oven and preheat to 500°F. Heavily dust a peel with cornmeal.

2. Tear cheese slices into pieces a few inches long. Tear basil leaves into a few pieces each.

3. Form dough into pizza crust and place on cornmeal-covered peel. Spread sauce over pizza. Arrange cheese pieces over top and drizzle olive oil over all.

4. Bake for 10 minutes or until edges are golden brown. Remove pizza from the oven, arrange basil leaves on top, cut into slices, and serve.

Variation: For **Deli Margherita Pizza,** replace mozzarella with 4 ounces sliced Swiss cheese and use **Sourdough Rye Pizza Dough.**

Secret Ingredient

You can thank nineteenth-century Italy's Queen Margherita for inspiring this creation. Her love of pizza helped move the dish beyond the realm of "peasant" food, and this pie was originally created in her honor. Be sure to use fresh basil on this pizza. Dried just doesn't work right. The Deli variation owes its name to the rye Swiss cheese combination you find in a New York deli sandwich.

Quattro Formaggio Pizza

A traditional style of Neapolitan pizza, the Italian name literally translates into "four cheeses."

1/8 cup ricotta cheese

1 oz. sliced provolone cheese

1/8 cup shredded mozzarella cheese

1/8 cup grated Parmesan cheese

Pizza Dough I, II, or III for 1 pizza (recipes/variations in Chapter 3)

1/3 cup Pomodoro Fresca Sauce (recipe in Chapter 5)

Yield: 1 pizza

Prep time:
15 minutes

Cook time:
10 minutes

Serving size:
1/3 to 1/2 pizza

1. Place a pizza stone or tiles in the oven and preheat to 500°F. Heavily dust a peel with cornmeal.

2. Tear cheese slices into pieces a few inches long.

3. Form dough into pizza crust and place on cornmeal-covered peel. Spread sauce over pizza. Scatter ricotta over top, and arrange provolone over all. Top with mozzarella and Parmesan.

Tips, Please

I go a bit light on the cheese to keep it from being overwhelming, but if you like more, add it on.

4. Bake for 10 minutes or until edges are golden brown. Remove pizza from the oven, cut into slices, and serve.

Caramelized Onion and Garlic Pizza

This pizza is reminiscent of a French Pissaladiere (recipe in Chapter 8) except on a thin crust and without the anchovies. There's no need for sauce; the sautéed onions add the moisture.

2 TB. olive oil

2 medium onions, cut into ¼-inch strips

1 tsp. kosher salt

3 cloves garlic, chopped

Pizza Dough I, II, or III for 1 pizza (recipes/variations in Chapter 3)

Yield: 1 pizza
Prep time: 15 minutes
Cook time: 20 minutes
Serving size: ⅓ to ½ pizza

1. Place a pizza stone or tiles in the oven and preheat to 500°F. Heavily dust a peel with cornmeal.

2. Heat a medium saucepan over medium heat, and add 2 tablespoons olive oil. Add onion strips, and cook until they turn a medium brown; some ends may be dark brown. Add more oil to the pan if it gets too dry. Add salt and garlic, and cook for 2 minutes longer or until garlic softens.

3. Form dough into pizza crust and place on cornmeal-covered peel. Spread onions onto pizza. Sprinkle with salt and remaining 1 tablespoon olive oil.

4. Bake for 10 minutes or until edges are golden brown. Remove pizza from the oven, cut into slices, and serve.

Tips, Please

For an extra taste boost, drizzle 1 tablespoon extra-virgin olive oil over the pizza right after it comes out of the oven.

Eggplant Pizza

You might find eggplant an unusual pizza topping, but after that first bite of eggplant, tomato sauce, and mozzarella cheese, you'll change your thinking.

1 small eggplant

2 tsp. kosher salt

Pizza Dough I, II, or III for 1 pizza (recipes/variations in Chapter 3)

1/3 cup Pomodoro Fresca Sauce (recipe in Chapter 5)

1/2 cup grated mozzarella cheese

1 TB. extra-virgin olive oil

Yield: 1 pizza
Prep time: 30 minutes
Cook time: 10 minutes
Serving size: 1/3 to 1/2 pizza

1. Place a pizza stone or tiles in the oven and preheat to 500°F. Heavily dust a peel with cornmeal.

2. Cut eggplant into 1/8-inch slices. Sprinkle with salt, and let rest about 25 minutes until drops of dark liquid appear. Rinse eggplant in cold water and pat dry.

3. Form dough into pizza crust and place on cornmeal-covered peel. Spread sauce over pizza. Sprinkle cheese on top. Arrange eggplant slices on top and sprinkle with remaining 1 teaspoon kosher salt. Sprinkle whole pizza with olive oil.

4. Bake for 10 minutes or until edges are golden brown. Remove pizza from the oven, cut into slices, and serve.

Secret Ingredient

Eggplant is a natural for pizzas. You salt the slices to draw out any potentially bitter liquid from the eggplant. Don't slice it too thinly, though, or the eggplant will turn to mush. And leave the peel on the eggplant; it adds color.

Brie and Artichoke Pizza

You'll notice I've not listed a sauce for this pizza. That's not an error. The creaminess of the Brie provides the moisture that would ordinarily come from a sauce.

4 oz. Brie

Sourdough Pizza Dough for 1 pizza (recipe in Chapter 3)

1 tsp. olive oil

½ tsp. kosher salt

¼ tsp. pepper

1 (10-oz.) pkg. frozen artichoke hearts, thawed

Yield: 1 pizza
Prep time: 15 minutes
Cook time: 10 minutes
Serving size: ⅓ to ½ pizza

1. Place a pizza stone or tiles in the oven and preheat to 500°F. Heavily dust a peel with cornmeal.

2. Trim crust off Brie, set aside, and slice cheese into thin slices.

3. Form dough into pizza crust and place on cornmeal-covered peel. Sprinkle surface first with olive oil and then with salt and pepper.

4. Bake pizza for 2 minutes. Remove from the oven. Place artichoke hearts over pizza and top with Brie slices. Arrange Brie crust slices on top.

5. Bake pizza another 8 minutes or until edges of pizza crust are deep golden brown, cut into slices, and serve.

Secret Ingredient

Don't toss that Brie crust after trimming it off the cheese. Brie crust is edible, and on top of the pizza it adds additional texture.

Spinach and Feta Pizza

Greeks found out long ago how well spinach, feta, and lemon juice work together. The result is a light yet satisfying pizza.

1 TB. olive oil

2 cloves garlic, crushed

½ (10-oz.) pkg. frozen chopped spinach, thawed

Oatmeal Pizza Dough for 1 pizza (recipe in Chapter 3)

4 oz. feta cheese, crumbled

⅓ cup White Sauce (recipe in Chapter 5; optional)

1 TB. lemon juice

Yield: 1 pizza
Prep time: 15 minutes
Cook time: 15 minutes
Serving size: ⅓ to ½ pizza

1. Place a pizza stone or tiles in the oven and preheat to 500°F. Heavily dust a peel with cornmeal.

2. Heat a medium pan over high heat, and add olive oil. Add garlic and cook until garlic starts to turn brown. Add spinach, toss to coat, and remove from heat.

3. Form dough into pizza crust and place on cornmeal-covered peel. Spread spinach on pizza, cover with sauce, and sprinkle with cheese. Drizzle lemon juice over all.

4. Bake for 10 minutes or until edges of crust are deep golden brown. Remove pizza from the oven, cut into slices, and serve.

Tips, Please

Add the sauce if you want, but try this recipe without it as well. If it seems too dry for your taste, you can also use extra lemon juice.

Chapter 8

Pizza Goes Global

In This Chapter

- ◆ Fun mini-pizza appetizers
- ◆ International flavor combinations
- ◆ Authentic Mexican pizza
- ◆ Hot day? Serve cold pizza

The idea of putting ingredients on some type of flatbread has a history thousands of years old and spanning many continents. The recipes in this chapter start making some of those international connections.

In some cases—the French *Pissaladiere* or the Mexican *Tlayuda*, for example—the dishes are traditional in their respective countries. In other cases, the combinations are interpretations of what international pizzas might be, with an eye to characteristic combinations of ingredients and spices.

Mexican *Tlayuda*

The corn tortilla crust paired with traditional Mexican ingredients like refried beans shows just how different pizza can be.

2 (6-in.) corn tortillas

½ cup refried beans

4 oz. shredded chicken, beef, or pork

⅔ cup chopped cabbage

½ cup grated Monterey Jack cheese

2 TB. Salsa (recipe in Chapter 5)

Yield: 2 tlayuda
Prep time: 5 minutes
Cook time: 6 minutes
Serving size: 1 tlayuda

1. Preheat the oven to 450°F.

2. Spread ¼ cup refried beans on each tortilla. Top each tortilla, in order, with half meat, cabbage, and cheese.

Doughfinition

The **tlayuda** is a dish, just coming to be known in the United States, that comes from Oaxaca, Mexico.

3. Place tortillas on a cookie sheet or in a roasting pan and bake 6 minutes or until tortillas are crisp and cheese melted. Remove tlayuda from the oven, top each with ½ of salsa, and serve.

French *Pissaladiere*

Even if you think you don't like anchovies, give this pizza a chance. The fish become milder after the milk bath and help add just enough salt to the onions, sweetened from the caramelizing.

Unbaked Focaccia dough (recipe in Chapter 3)

4 TB. olive oil

2 (2-oz.) cans anchovy flat fillets, drained

½ cup milk

1 large onion

2 cloves garlic, minced

25 pitted kalamata olives or pitted medium black olives, halved

1 TB. kosher salt

Yield: 1 pizza
Prep time: 30 minutes
Cook time: 45 minutes
Serving size: ⅛ pizza

1. Preheat the empty oven to 375°F.

2. Using a rolling pin, roll out dough so it's the dimensions of the bottom of a 17¼×11½×1-inch baking pan. Grease inside of pan with 1 tablespoon olive oil. Lift dough into pan. Let rise until almost doubled in bulk.

3. While dough is rising, place anchovy fillets in a small, flat container. Add milk, gently separate fillets, and set aside to soak for 20 minutes.

4. Trim top and bottom of onion, and split onion in half through root end. For each half, put cut side flat on a cutting board. Make a few horizontal cuts about ¼ inch apart through onion, stopping them just before you cut through root end. Next, make a few vertical cuts ¼ inch apart, again stopping just before root end. Finally, cut off root end separate half into ¼×¼-inch strips.

5. Heat a large frying pan over high heat and add 2 tablespoons olive oil. Add onion, sautéing until translucent. Add garlic and cook until it softens. Remove from heat.

6. With your fingertips, make small indentations over the entire surface of dough. Spread cooked onions and garlic over surface, leaving 1/2-inch border. Arrange anchovy filets diagonally in both directions within border to make a diamond lattice. Put an olive half in the center of each diamond. Sprinkle surface with remaining 1 tablespoon olive oil and salt.

Doughfinition

A **pissaladiere** is a French-style pizza that comes from Provence. It's a great snack or light meal.

7. Bake for 35 minutes or until border is golden brown and onions are partly browned. Using a spatula, remove pissaladiere from pan, cut into squares, and serve.

Spanish Tapas Pizza

Tapas, Spanish for "small plates," are the appetizers you find in bars in Spain. These bite-size pizzas are the literal interpretation, as you eat the small dough "plates."

Any full pizza dough recipe (recipe in Chapter 3)

Toppings:

1 tsp. mashed sweet potatoes and 1 *cornichon*

½ tsp. Cocktail Sauce (recipe in Chapter 5) and 1 small shrimp

1 TB. tuna salad topped with 2×¼-in. strip pickled *pimiento* and 1 pickled cocktail onion

1 TB. mix of 2 parts egg salad and 1 part grated *Manchego* cheese (place pizzas under the broiler until cheese melts)

2 cooked and cooled mussels topped with a strip of lemon zest (cut with a vegetable peeler, avoiding white pith)

1 TB. mushroom topping from Mushroom Pizza (variation in Chapter 7)

1 artichoke bottom (canned) filled with 1½ tsp. green peas and 2 tsp. cheese sauce

2 tsp. chopped green olives, topped with 1 tsp. mascarpone and ⅛ tsp. chopped chives

1 TB. salad tossed with vinaigrette dressing and topped with 1 (⅛-in.) slice water chestnut

Yield: 50 appetizer pizzas
Prep time: 30 minutes
Cook time: 5 minutes
Serving size: 3 pizzas

1. Preheat the empty oven to 500°F. Spray 2 cookie sheets with cooking oil spray.

2. Divide dough in half, divide each half into 5 pieces, and divide each of those pieces into 5 dough balls. Using a rolling pin, roll out each ball so it's about 2 inches across. Pinch in around each circle to create a bunched-up edge about ¼-inch tall.

3. Place 25 rounds on each cookie sheet, and bake for about 5 minutes or until golden brown. Remove and allow to cool.

4. Top each round with your choice of toppings and serve.

Doughfinition

A **cornichon** is the French version of the gherkin pickle, though typically smaller than the U.S. style. **Pimiento** is a Spanish-style pepper usually sold roasted, skinned, and pickled. **Manchego** is a Spanish cheese that can be either semi-soft or hard and made of either cow or sheep milk.

Indian Pizza

The topping for this dish is a mild version of an Indian dish often served with naan, so it only seemed right to pair the two.

12 oz. boneless skinless chicken tenders

½ tsp. salt

2 TB. olive oil

1 (10-oz.) pkg. frozen chopped spinach, thawed

2 cloves garlic

2 TB. freshly grated ginger

2 TB. heavy cream

1 TB. plain yogurt

12 pieces Naan bread (1 batch, recipe in Chapter 3)

Yield: 12 pizzas
Prep time: 15 minutes
Cook time: 22 minutes
Serving size: 2 pizzas

1. Preheat the broiler.

2. Slice chicken tenders into pieces about 1 inch long and sprinkle with salt.

3. Heat a medium pan over high heat, and add 1 tablespoon olive oil. Add chicken and cook until it turns opaque. Remove the pan from heat and reserve chicken.

4. Put spinach, garlic, and ginger into a blender or food processor. Blend or process until smooth.

5. Heat a pan over high heat, and add remaining 1 tablespoon oil. When hot, add spinach mixture and cook for 1 minute. Reduce heat to simmer, add cream and yogurt, and cook for 10 minutes. Return chicken to the pan, and simmer for 5 minutes.

6. Split chicken and spinach mixture evenly among naan breads, topping each one and leaving a ¼-inch border around the edge. Place on a cookie sheet and heat under the broiler for 1 minute. Serve.

Secret Ingredient

Monica Bhide, a friend and author of *The Spice Is Right: Easy Indian Cooking for Today*, knew I was writing this book and mentioned that her family often added toppings to naan. That was as knowledgeable a recommendation as I could get.

Scandinavian Pizza

Rye bread, beets, herring, and dill are often found in Scandinavian cooking—and this pizza.

Rye Pizza Dough for 1 pizza (variation in Chapter 3)

⅓ lb. pickled herring in either sour cream or wine sauce

⅓ cup sour cream

1 tsp. grated horseradish

⅓ cup sliced pickled beets

2 tsp. chopped dill

Yield: 1 pizza
Prep time:
15 minutes
Cook time:
10 minutes
Serving size:
⅓ to ½ pizza

1. Place a pizza stone or tiles in the oven and preheat to 500°F. Heavily dust a peel with cornmeal.

2. Form dough into pizza crust and place on cornmeal-covered peel. Bake for 10 minutes or until golden brown. Remove from the oven and allow to cool.

3. Cut herring into roughly 1-inch pieces and set aside.

4. Mix sour cream and horseradish, and spread over pizza. Arrange herring and beet slices over top, and sprinkle with dill. Cut into slices and serve.

Secret Ingredient

Many different types of pickled herring are available in northern Europe, where the preserved fish is popular. In U.S. grocery stores, you'll generally find two types: in wine sauce or in sour cream.

Middle Eastern Pizza

The mint and other refreshing ingredients make this cold pizza a good choice for hot weather.

1 (5- or 6-in.) pita bread

1/2 cup *hummus*

1/2 cup *tabbouleh*

8 stuffed grape leaves (available in cans or at some deli counters)

1 TB. chopped fresh mint

Yield: 2 pizzas
Prep time:
15 minutes
Cook time:
2 minutes
Serving size:
1 pizza

1. Place a pizza stone or tiles in the oven and preheat to 500°F.

2. Insert a knife into edge of pita and cut around entire circumference, splitting pita into 2 discs. Put both on a cookie sheet, cut side up, and bake until crisp, about 2 minutes. Remove from the oven and allow to cool.

3. Spread each pita half with hummus and tabbouleh. Arrange 4 grape leaves on each half, sprinkle chopped mint on top, and serve.

Doughfinition

Tabbouleh is a Middle Eastern salad with chopped tomatoes, parsley, mint, and bulgur wheat. **Hummus** is a thick Middle Eastern spread made of puréed garbanzo beans, lemon juice, olive oil, garlic, and often tahini (sesame seed paste).

German Pizza

This pizza variation is a fun change from having knockwurst on a plate or in a bun.

Rye Pizza Dough for 1 pizza (variation in Chapter 3)

⅓ lb. knockwurst

⅛ cup brown mustard

⅓ cup sauerkraut, drained

¼ lb. thin slices muenster cheese

Yield: 1 pizza
Prep time:
15 minutes
Cook time:
10 minutes
Serving size:
⅓ to ½ pizza

1. Place a pizza stone or tiles in the oven and preheat to 500°F. Heavily dust a peel with cornmeal.

2. Slice knockwurst into ⅛-inch slices.

3. Form dough into pizza crust and place on cornmeal-covered peel. Spread mustard over crust and evenly arrange sauerkraut over top. Top with knockwurst and cheese slices.

4. Bake for 10 minutes, or until edge crust is golden and cheese melted. Remove pizza from the oven, cut into slices, and serve.

 Tips, Please

If you find the taste of sauerkraut too strong, soak it in cold water for 5 minutes and then drain before using.

Greek Pizza

The ingredients and approach might be just as suited to a batch of the Greek eggplant dish called moussaka.

Pizza Dough I, II, or III, or Sourdough Pizza Dough for 1 pizza (recipes/variations in Chapter 3)

⅓ lb. ground lamb

¼ cup Pomodoro Fresca Sauce (recipe in Chapter 5)

⅓ cup Greek Egg-Enriched White Sauce (variation in Chapter 5)

¼ cup pitted kalamata olives, cut in ½

¼ cup crumbled feta cheese

Yield: 1 pizza
Prep time: 30 minutes
Cook time: 20 minutes
Serving size: ⅓ to ½ pizza

1. Preheat the oven to 500°F.

2. Form dough into pizza crust and place in a 9-inch cake pan. Bake for 2 minutes and remove from the oven.

3. In medium pan over medium heat, cook lamb, breaking up any lumps.

4. Spread pizza with Pomodoro Fresca Sauce and then add lamb. Cover with white sauce, and top with olives and cheese.

5. Bake for 8 minutes or until edges are golden and cheese melted. Remove pizza from the oven, cut into slices, and serve.

Variation: For **Vegetarian Greek Pizza,** instead of lamb, slice a small eggplant into ⅛-inch rounds. Cook them in a large pan with 2 tablespoons olive oil for about 2 minutes per side, turning once. Arrange eggplant slices on the pizza instead of the ground lamb and continue as directed.

Secret Ingredient

In Massachusetts, many pizza shops are run by Greek families. All the pizzas are made in pans with an effect halfway between a regular pie and a deep-dish one.

Russian Pizza

This recipe uses a buckwheat crust and substitutes a beef Stroganoff–like topping.

Buckwheat Pizza Dough for 1 pizza (variation in Chapter 3)

1 TB. olive oil

½ small onion, sliced paper thin

⅓ cup beef stock

1½ tsp. butter

1½ tsp. all-purpose flour

2 TB. sour cream

Salt

⅓ lb. beef tenderloin or sirloin steak, sliced paper thin

> **Yield: 1 pizza**
>
> **Prep time:**
> 15 minutes
>
> **Cook time:**
> 10 minutes
>
> **Serving size:**
> ⅓ to ½ pizza

1. Place a pizza stone or tiles in the oven and preheat to 500°F. Heavily dust a peel with cornmeal.

2. Form dough into pizza crust and place on cornmeal-covered peel.

3. Heat a medium pan over medium heat, and add olive oil. Add onion and sauté until translucent. Drain and set aside.

4. Heat beef stock in a medium pot over medium heat until hot but not boiling.

5. In a medium saucepan over high heat, melt butter. Add flour and cook until light brown. Add stock and whisk until blended. Cook 5 minutes or until sauce thickens. Remove from heat, blend in sour cream, and season with salt.

6. Spread sauce on pizza. Scatter cooked onions on top. Arrange beef slices over all.

7. Bake for 10 minutes or until edges are golden brown. Remove pizza from the oven, cut into slices, and serve.

Secret Ingredient

Buckwheat pancakes are a traditional base for caviar; however, that makes for one expensive snack.

Chapter 9

Pizza in the Morning

In This Chapter

- ◆ Breakfast for everyone, at the same time
- ◆ Wake up to a bacon and egg custard–topped pizza
- ◆ In the mood for a spicy Mexican breakfast?
- ◆ Start the day with a sweet pie

Mention pizza as a breakfast food and most people assume you're about to serve cold leftovers from last night's takeout. But pizza is a natural for the first meal of the day. Some of these recipes come from traditions in countries where people see the wisdom of pairing flatbreads and toppings.

If you do want to serve a pizza in the morning, make the dough late the preceding day and put it into an oiled plastic bag as though you were going to freeze it (see Chapter 2), but instead put it into the fridge so it won't need to thaw before you make breakfast.

Vegetable Scramble Pizza

Feel free to eat this veggie-topped pizza with your fingers with no disapproval from the folks.

Pizza Dough I, II, or III (recipes/variations in Chapter 3)

1 TB. water

1 TB. olive oil

½ cup diced green bell pepper

½ cup diced onion

½ cup sliced mushrooms

6 eggs

¼ lb. Monterey Jack cheese, grated

Yield: 1 pizza
Prep time:
30 minutes
Cook time:
15 minutes
Serving size:
¼ pizza

1. Place a pizza stone or tiles in the oven, and preheat the oven to 500°F. Heavily dust a peel with cornmeal.

2. Form dough into pizza crust and place on cornmeal-covered peel. Bake 5 minutes and remove from oven. Return to the peel.

3. In large frying pan over medium heat, heat oil. Add green bell pepper and onion, and cook until onion is translucent. Add mushrooms, and cook until mushrooms soften.

4. In a large bowl, beat eggs with water. Add eggs to the pan, and cook until eggs set but still very soft.

5. Transfer eggs to pizza crust, sprinkle cheese on top, and bake 10 minutes or until crust edge is golden brown and cheese melts. Serve.

Tips, Please

This scramble pizza lets you serve a number of people without having to wait for each person's breakfast to come off the stove. If you want, you can add ½ cup diced cooked ham with the mushrooms.

Flaeskeaeggekage Pizza (Bacon and Egg Cake Pizza)

Traditionally, this dish is served in Denmark without a crust, directly from the pan in which it cooked.

2 tsp. olive oil

Rye Pizza Dough for 1 pizza (variation in Chapter 3)

¼ lb. bacon, cut into 1-inch pieces

6 large eggs

1 cup whole or 2% milk

2 TB. vegetable oil

½ tsp. salt

2 TB. chopped chives

Yield: 1 pizza
Prep time: 30 minutes
Cook time: 35 minutes
Serving size: ¼ pizza

1. Preheat the oven to 350°F. Coat inside of a 9-inch cake pan with olive oil and line the pan with pizza dough.

2. In a skillet over medium heat, cook bacon until cooked through. Drain on paper towels. When drained, arrange bacon on pizza dough.

3. In a large bowl, beat eggs with milk and salt until completely blended. Pour over bacon on pizza.

4. Put the cake pan in the oven, and bake for 25 minutes or until a knife blade inserted into the middle of filling comes out clean. Top with chives and serve.

Doughfinition

A *flaeskeaeggekage* is like a Danish version of quiche, but with a more custardlike consistency.

Huevos Rancheros

For a spicy way to start your day, you can't go wrong with the ever-popular Huevos Rancheros. This is a great weekend breakfast recipe, too. Get the whole family involved in the cooking.

2 (6-in.) tortillas

2 TB. refried beans

2 tsp. butter

2 large eggs

2 TB. Salsa (recipe in Chapter 5)

2 tsp. sour cream

2 tsp. guacamole

Yield: 1 serving
Prep time: 20 minutes
Cook time: 15 minutes
Serving size: 2 tortillas

1. Place a pizza stone or tiles in the oven, and preheat the oven to 500°F.

2. Heat tortillas in the oven directly on the stone or tiles until tortillas are crisp and then remove. Spread 1 tablespoon refried beans on each tortilla.

3. In a frying pan over medium heat, melt butter. Add eggs and fry until done. Put 1 egg on each tortilla. Top each egg with 1 tablespoon salsa. Garnish with sour cream and guacamole, and serve.

 Secret Ingredient

Huevos rancheros, or "ranch-style" eggs, are an old favorite in Mexican and Tex-Mex cuisines.

Fruit and Oatmeal Pizza

With the fruit and yogurt topping the Sweet Oatmeal crust, you could serve this breakfast pizza for dessert.

Sweet Oatmeal Pizza Dough for 1 pizza (variation in Chapter 3)

1 cup vanilla yogurt

1½ cups sliced fruit (your favorite)

2 TB. sugar

Yield: 1 pizza
Prep time: 20 minutes
Cook time: 10 minutes
Serving size: ¼ pizza

1. Place a pizza stone or tiles in the oven, and preheat the oven to 500°F. Line a 9-inch cake pan with pizza dough. Bake for 8 minutes or until crust is golden and then remove from the oven.

2. Spread yogurt on pizza. Arrange fruit on top, and sift sugar over fruit.

3. Set oven to broil. Put pizza under broiler until sugar caramelizes, remove, and serve.

Tips, Please

If you have one of those handheld blow torches used in kitchens to caramelize sugar sprinkled on a dessert, feel free to use it. If you don't, the boiler works just the same.

Streusel Pizza

Streusel refers to the butter and sugar mix used in many pastry recipes. That, combined with the Caramel Sauce and cinnamon, makes this a sweet pizza that could do double-duty as a dessert if you like.

¼ cup brown sugar

1 TB. all-purpose flour

½ tsp. cinnamon

4 TB. butter

Sweet Pizza Dough for 1 pizza (variation in Chapter 3)

½ cup Caramel Sauce (recipe in Chapter 5)

½ cup chopped walnuts (or your favorite)

Yield: 1 pizza
Prep time:
20 minutes
Cook time:
10 minutes
Serving size:
¼ pizza

1. Place a pizza stone or tiles in the oven, and preheat the oven to 500°F. Heavily dust a peel with cornmeal.

2. In a small bowl, combine brown sugar, flour, and cinnamon. Add butter, and mix until the consistency of breadcrumbs.

3. Form dough into pizza crust, and place on cornmeal-covered peel. Bake pizza for 2 minutes and then remove from the oven.

4. Spread Caramel Sauce on pizza, arrange chopped nuts on top, and sprinkle sugar and butter mixture over all. Bake 8 minutes or until crust is golden brown and serve.

Secret Ingredient

This is a bit sweet for breakfast, I admit, but then so are coffee cake and sticky buns, so the recipe has good company. If you feel guilty, add ½ cup fresh fruit slices right after spreading on the Caramel Sauce.

Between a Roll and a Hot Place

On a cold day and with a cup of soup, a hot panino can really hit the spot—talk about comfort food. Or on a hot day, a cool panino can be just as refreshing. If either sounds good to you, you've come to the right part of the book. What Part 3 did for pizzas, Part 4 does for panini. Here you'll find meaty as well as veggie panini, panini from around the globe, and breakfast panini.

Chapter 10

Carnivore Combos

In This Chapter

◆ Tips for cooking panini fillings

◆ Last night's leftovers? Today's panino!

◆ Find panini inspiration in all sorts of interesting dishes around you

Meat sandwiches are fine, but it's easy to become so accustomed to them that you don't even taste what you're having after a while.

Let a panino change your culinary outlook. The grilled texture of the bread offers a good counterpoint to the fillings, and when you're going to the trouble of breaking out a grill, chances are, you'll consider other ingredients to make something extraordinary out of the ordinary.

Another good thing about panini is that they're economical. You can fill them with leftover roast, steak, chicken, or anything else you might have, and because you only need to make one sandwich, you can use up the last bits of dinner over the next few days.

A Few Panini Tips

If you do plan to cook something for a sandwich filling, plan it ahead of time so you're not setting aside hours for a single sandwich.

Note that throughout the next few chapters, heating the grill means, for electric models, simply turning them on. For stove-top units, heat the grill over medium heat until it is hot.

Remember as well that you don't need to bake your own bread. Buy a loaf and use a couple slices if you want, or get a roll and split it for the sandwich.

Secret Ingredient

While you certainly can purchase bread or rolls for your panino, why not take the extra few steps and bake your own bread? It'll make your sandwich that much better, plus you'll often have leftover bread you can use for other panini or French toast or even just butter and bread when you want a sweet snack.

Salami, Provolone, and Roasted Bell Pepper Panino

This panino is probably close to one you might find in Italy—simple and not too thickly filled.

2 slices Ciabatta (recipe in Chapter 4)

1½ tsp. olive oil

1 tsp. Italian salad dressing

⅛ lb. thinly sliced salami

3 slices provolone cheese

4 slices Roasted Bell Pepper (recipe in Chapter 5)

Yield: 1 panino
Prep time: 15 minutes
Cook time: 5 minutes
Serving size: 1 panino

1. Heat the grill.

2. Spread outside faces of bread with ¾ teaspoon olive oil each. Spread one inside face with Italian dressing.

3. Assemble sandwich with salami, provolone, and roasted red pepper. Grill sandwich 5 minutes or until outside faces are golden brown. Serve.

Secret Ingredient

For a more assertive flavor, you can use raw red bell pepper—or any other color, for that matter.

Lamb and Chevre Panino

The chevre adds tang to the common pairing of lamb and mint.

2 slices Oatmeal Bread (recipe in Chapter 4)

1½ tsp. olive oil

2 tsp. mint jelly

2 TB. *chevre*

⅛ lb. sliced cooked lamb (roast or chops)

2 thin slices red onion

Yield: 1 panino
Prep time:
15 minutes
Cook time:
5 minutes
Serving size:
1 panino

1. Heat the grill.

2. Spread outside faces of bread with ¾ teaspoon olive oil each. Spread one inside face of bread with mint jelly. Spread other inside face with chevre.

3. Assemble sandwich with lamb and onion. Grill sandwich 5 minutes or until outside faces are golden brown. Serve.

Doughfinition

Chevre is French for "goat milk cheese" and is typically creamy, salty, and soft. Chevres are delicious alone or paired with fruits or chutney. Chevres vary in style from mild and creamy to aged, firm, and flavorful.

Sausage, Onion, and Fruit Panino

This is a good sandwich for a cold autumn day. The fruit pairs nicely with the sausage and onion flavors.

¼ lb. cooked mild Italian sausage

2 slices Ciabatta (recipe in Chapter 4)

1½ tsp. olive oil

2 thin slices onion

¼ pear, thinly sliced

¼ apple, thinly sliced

2 tsp. chopped walnuts

Yield: 1 panino
Prep time:
15 minutes
Cook time:
5 minutes
Serving size:
1 panino

1. Heat the grill.
2. Slice sausage on the diagonal into ⅛-inch oval pieces and set aside.
3. Spread outside faces of bread with ¾ teaspoon olive oil each.
4. Assemble sandwich with sausage, onion, pear, apple, and walnuts. Grill sandwich 5 minutes or until outside faces are golden brown. Serve.

Secret Ingredient

I've been refining my Thanksgiving stuffing recipe over the years. The basic elements are all here, so now there's no need to wait for it to appear in a bird.

Reuben Panino

I'm sure you're familiar with the Reuben, the masterpiece of delicatessen fare. This version has all your favorite flavors on delicious sourdough rye bread.

2 slices Sourdough Rye Bread (recipe in Chapter 4)

1½ tsp. butter

1 TB. Russian or Thousand Island salad dressing

¼ lb. corned beef

⅓ cup sauerkraut, drained

2 slices Swiss cheese

Yield: 1 panino
Prep time: 15 minutes
Cook time: 5 minutes
Serving size: 1 panino

1. Heat the grill.

2. Spread outside faces of bread with ¾ teaspoon butter each. Spread one inside face with Russian dressing.

Secret Ingredient

I enjoy this sandwich so much, I developed a Reuben Pizza recipe, too (see Chapter 6).

3. Assemble sandwich with corned beef on bare inside bread face followed by sauerkraut and cheese. Grill sandwich 5 minutes or until outside faces are golden brown and cheese melts. Serve.

Oyster Po'Boy Panino

The po'boy is a New Orleans native that shows it's possible to eat well even without real silverware and vintage wine.

¹/₂ cup shelled oysters

¹/₂ cup buttermilk

2 cups vegetable oil

2 slices Ciabatta (recipe in Chapter 4)

1¹/₂ tsp. olive oil

¹/₂ TB. mayonnaise

¹/₂ TB. Creole or stone ground Dijon mustard

¹/₃ cup all-purpose flour

¹/₂ tsp. salt

¹/₄ tsp. pepper

1 large egg

1 TB. water

¹/₃ cup cornmeal

¹/₄ cup sweet pickle slices

3 slices tomato

¹/₂ cup shredded cabbage or shredded lettuce

Yield: 1 panino
Prep time:
15 minutes, plus overnight for soaking
Cook time:
10 minutes
Serving size:
1 panino

1. The evening before you'll want the sandwich, place oysters in a bowl. Add buttermilk and place in the refrigerator to soak.

2. The next day, heat the grill.

3. In a medium pot over high heat, heat vegetable oil to 375°F.

4. Cut bread almost through, leaving a hinge. Spread outside faces of bread with ¾ teaspoon olive oil each. Spread bottom inside face with mayonnaise and top inside face with mustard.

5. Put flour in a bowl and add salt and pepper. In another bowl, beat egg with water. In a third bowl, add cornmeal.

Secret Ingredient

Setting up for deep-frying shellfish is a bit time-consuming and potentially messy, so use a dedicated deep fryer if you have one and plan on making this for company so you don't go to the trouble for just one.

6. Drain oysters and dredge in flour mix, shaking off any excess flour. Dip in egg mix and then dredge in cornmeal. Fry coated oysters in oil until golden brown. Remove and drain.

7. Assemble sandwich starting on bottom with pickle slices, tomato slices, cabbage, and fried oysters. Grill sandwich 5 minutes or until outside faces are golden brown. Serve.

Salmon and Spinach Panino

Not only do the salmon, mango chutney, spinach, and oatmeal flavors complement one another, but wait until you see colors.

2 slices Oatmeal Bread (recipe in Chapter 4)

1½ tsp. olive oil

1 TB. mango chutney

¼ lb. cooked salmon fillet

½ cup cooked spinach

Yield: 1 panino
Prep time:
5 minutes
Cook time:
5 minutes
Serving size:
1 panino

1. Heat the grill.

2. Spread outsides face of bread with ¾ teaspoon olive oil each. Spread one inside face with mango chutney.

3. Cut salmon across fillet to make slices.

4. Assemble sandwich with salmon slices and spinach. Grill sandwich 5 minutes or until outside faces are golden. Serve.

Tips, Please

Most Americans don't stock chutney in their pantries, but maybe you should. I find it a wonderful and versatile condiment, whether having Indian *aloo palak* or a burger.

Brisket and Gravy Panino

With a combination of brisket, gravy, Swiss cheese, and sourdough bread, this panino is very worthy of the "sticks to your ribs" description.

2 slices Sourdough Bread (recipe in Chapter 4)

1½ tsp. olive oil

1 TB. brisket gravy or Beef Gravy (recipe in Chapter 5)

¼ lb. cooked beef brisket

2 slices Swiss cheese

¼ cup onions cooked with brisket

Yield: 1 panino
Prep time: 25 minutes
Cook time: 5 minutes
Serving size: 1 panino

1. Heat the grill.

2. Spread outside faces of bread with ¾ teaspoon olive oil each. Spread one inside face with gravy.

3. Cut brisket into ⅛-inch slices.

4. Assemble sandwich with brisket slices, cheese, and onions. Grill sandwich 5 minutes or until outside faces are golden and cheese melts. Serve.

Variation: If you didn't cook onions in with the brisket, you can substitute sautéed or raw onions in this recipe.

Secret Ingredient

Many years ago, in a small sandwich shop in Cambridge, Massachusetts, called Elsie's, I ordered a brisket with gravy and onions, and someone behind the counter suggested adding some Swiss cheese. I did and never looked back.

Roast Beef and Havarti Panino

Roast beef and havarti is a combination often ordered in sandwich shops. The horseradish adds bite, and the cucumber provides a contrast in texture.

2 slices Sourdough Rye Bread (recipe in Chapter 4)

1½ tsp. olive oil

1 tsp. prepared horseradish

¼ lb. sliced cooked roast beef

Salt and pepper

2 slices Havarti cheese

4 slices cucumber

Yield: 1 panino
Prep time:
15 minutes
Cook time:
5 minutes
Serving size:
1 panino

1. Heat the grill.

2. Spread outside faces of bread with ¾ teaspoon olive oil each. Spread one inside face of bread with horseradish.

3. Put roast beef on bread, season with salt and pepper, and top with cheese and cucumber slices. Grill sandwich 5 minutes or until outside faces are golden and cheese melts. Serve.

Tips, Please

Use prepared horseradish because grating the root is one of the most unpleasant kitchen tasks, making chopping strong onions seem like a leisure activity.

Day-After-Thanksgiving Panino

When you are running out of ways to use holiday leftovers, here's a new possibility. It's got all the flavors of Thanksgiving—turkey, gravy, even cranberry sauce—all in one panino.

2 slices Ciabatta (recipe in Chapter 4)

1½ tsp. olive oil

1 TB. leftover gravy (optional)

1 TB. cranberry sauce

¼ lb. sliced cooked turkey

2 slices Swiss cheese

Yield: 1 panino
Prep time: 15 minutes
Cook time: 5 minutes
Serving size: 1 panino

1. Heat the grill.

2. Spread outside faces of bread with ¾ teaspoon olive oil each. Spread one inside face with gravy (if using) and the other with cranberry sauce.

3. Assemble turkey and cheese on sandwich. Grill sandwich 5 minutes or until outside faces are golden and cheese melts. Serve.

Secret Ingredient

Recipes for using holiday leftovers are always handy. After trying this, you'll make more turkey just to have the leftovers for this panino.

Tuna Meltdown Panino

Tuna salad plus Guoda cheese plus avocado—you won't believe all the flavors packed in this panino.

2 slices Ciabatta (recipe in Chapter 4)

1½ tsp. olive oil

½ cup tuna salad (homemade or from the deli)

2 slices *Gouda* cheese

4 slices avocado

Yield: 1 panino
Prep time: 15 minutes
Cook time: 5 minutes
Serving size: 1 panino

1. Heat the grill.

2. Spread outside faces of bread with ¾ teaspoon olive oil each.

3. Assemble tuna salad, cheese, and avocado slices on sandwich. Grill sandwich 5 minutes or until outside faces are golden and cheese melts. Serve.

Variation: For a more complex flavor, add a few drops of hot pepper sauce.

Doughfinition

Gouda is a mild Dutch cheese made from cow's milk.

BLCT Panino

If you're a fan of BLTs and also like cheese, this panino is for you.

2 slices Oatmeal Bread (recipe in Chapter 4)

1½ tsp. olive oil

2 slices Havarti cheese

4 slices cooked bacon

2 slices tomato

½ cup mixed greens

Yield: 1 panino
Prep time: 15 minutes
Cook time: 5 minutes
Serving size: 1 panino

1. Heat the grill.

2. Spread outside faces of bread with ¾ teaspoon olive oil each.

3. Assemble cheese, bacon, tomato, and mixed greens on sandwich. Grill sandwich 5 minutes or until outside faces are golden and cheese melts. Serve.

Doughfinition

Havarti is a creamy, Danish, mild cow's milk cheese perhaps most enjoyed in its herbed versions such as Havarti with dill.

Ham, Cheddar, and Apple Panino

Ham and cheddar are flavors often paired, so you're probably familiar with that combination. You might think the apple strange, but wait until you taste it.

2 slices Sweet Oatmeal Bread (variation in Chapter 4)

1½ tsp. olive oil

2 tsp. maple syrup

¼ lb. sliced ham

2 slices cheddar cheese

¼ apple, cored and sliced into ⅛-inch slices

Yield: 1 panino
Prep time: 15 minutes
Cook time: 5 minutes
Serving size: 1 panino

1. Heat the grill.

2. Spread outside faces of bread with ¾ teaspoon olive oil each. Spread one inside face with maple syrup.

3. Assemble ham, cheese, and apple on sandwich. Grill sandwich 5 minutes or until outside faces are golden and cheese melts. Serve.

Secret Ingredient

I live in a part of the country where apples and maple syrup are important to the local economy. A local breakfast and lunch counter actually combined most of these ingredients into a sandwich, which is where I got the idea.

Chapter 11

Plant-Filled Panini

In This Chapter

- ◆ Use your grill to cook vegetables
- ◆ Vegetables leftovers? Veggie panini!
- ◆ Celebrate the seasons with vegetable sandwiches
- ◆ Tip on veggie prep

Meats aren't the only items you can put into a sandwich. Combining cheeses, vegetables, and fruits creates a world of variety, giving you meals light yet still filling.

Vegetables and fruits even offer greater versatility than meat in terms of what you can do. Sometimes you use them raw for one effect or cook them in advance to get another. Panini also give you another way to use leftover vegetables.

Grilled Eggplant Panino

The grilled eggplant in this panino practically melts in your mouth.

⅛ lb. eggplant

1 TB. kosher salt

1 TB. plus 1½ tsp. olive oil

3 slices Parmigiano Reggiano cheese

2 slices Ciabatta (recipe in Chapter 4)

1 tsp. Italian salad dressing

Yield: 1 panino
Prep time: 30 minutes
Cook time: 20 minutes
Serving size: 1 panino

1. Cut eggplant into ⅛-inch slices. Sprinkle both sides with salt, and let rest 30 minutes or until drops of dark liquid appear. Rinse eggplant in cold water and pat dry. Although it's not necessary, you can peel the eggplant if you prefer it that way.

2. Heat the grill. Brush eggplant slices with 1 tablespoon olive oil and grill on each side until slices are softened and faces are partly browned.

Hot Stuff

Don't substitute already grated Parmesan for the Parmigiano Reggiano. The flavor and texture are too important to settle for the pre-shredded stuff. (Slice it with a vegetable shredder—easy.)

3. Spread outside faces of bread with ¾ teaspoon olive oil each. Spread one inside face with Italian dressing. Assemble sandwich with eggplant and cheese. Grill sandwich 5 minutes or until outside faces are golden brown and cheese is melted. Serve.

Caprese Panino

Insalada Caprese is a type of Italian salad with mozzerella, tomato, and basil. This is the sandwich version.

2 slices Ciabatta (recipe in Chapter 4)

1½ tsp. olive oil

¼ lb. mozzarella cheese

4 slices tomato

4 to 6 fresh basil leaves

½ tsp. balsamic vinegar

Yield: 1 panino
Prep time: 15 minutes
Cook time: 5 minutes
Serving size: 1 panino

1. Heat the grill.

2. Cut bread in half, and spread outside faces with ¾ teaspoon olive oil each. Spread 1 inside face of bread with balsamic vinegar.

3. Assemble sandwich with cheese, tomato slices, and enough basil leaves to cover sandwich. Grill sandwich 5 minutes or until outside faces are crisp and cheese is melted. Serve.

 Secret Ingredient

The red, green, and white colors mirror those of Italy's flag.

Roasted Fennel Panino

Fennel has a spicy anise flavor that works well with the tang of the chevre and naan.

¼ lb. fennel bulb

1 TB. extra-virgin olive oil

1 tsp. kosher salt

¼ lb. chevre

1 Naan bread (recipe in Chapter 3)

1½ tsp. olive oil

2 tsp. raspberry vinaigrette or any other fruit-flavored salad dressing

½ cup mixed greens

Yield: 1 panino
Prep time:
45 minutes
Cook time:
25 minutes
Serving size:
1 panino

1. Preheat the oven to 450°F. Heat the grill.

2. Cut fennel bulb lengthwise into ¼-inch slices. Place into roasting pan, cover with extra-virgin olive oil, and stir slices to coat all of each piece. Arrange in single layer on roasting pan, sprinkle with salt, and roast 20 minutes or until slices soften and edges turn medium brown. Remove from the oven and reserve.

3. Cut chevre into ¼-inch slices.

Tips, Please

Use trimmings from the top of the fennel bulb to add the anise taste to other dishes.

4. Split naan, and spread outside faces with ¾ teaspoon olive oil each. Sprinkle top inside with vinaigrette.

5. Assemble sandwich with fennel slices, chevre slices, and mixed greens. Grill sandwich 5 minutes or until outside faces are crisp and cheese is melted. Serve.

Peach and Carrot Panino

A tasty sandwich for summer, the peach and carrot pair nicely with the Oatmeal Bread.

1 peach

2 slices Oatmeal Bread (recipe in Chapter 4)

1½ tsp. olive oil

1 TB. pepper jelly

½ cup shredded carrot

Yield: 1 panino
Prep time:
15 minutes
Cook time:
5 minutes
Serving size:
1 panino

1. Heat the grill.

2. Cut peach into halves, remove pit, and cut peach into ¼-inch slices.

3. Spread outside faces of bread with ¾ teaspoon olive oil each. Spread pepper jelly on top inside.

4. Assemble sandwich with peach slices and shredded carrot. Grill sandwich 5 minutes or until outside faces are golden brown. Serve.

Doughfinition

Pepper jelly is a type of prepared jelly, found in many grocery stores and specialty food shops, incorporating peppers. It may be a sweet pepper or hot type.

Asparagus and Sun-Dried Tomato Panino

This is a good sandwich for spring, when the brief domestic asparagus season makes prices reasonable for a few weeks.

4 spears asparagus, stem bottoms trimmed

2 slices Sourdough Rye Bread (recipe in Chapter 4)

1½ tsp. olive oil

1 tsp. herb-flavored vinegar (rosemary or any other)

⅛ tsp. red pepper flakes (optional)

4 sun-dried tomatoes in oil

Yield: 1 panino
Prep time: 30 minutes
Cook time: 15 minutes
Serving size: 1 panino

1. Heat the grill.

2. Heat a frying pan over high heat with enough water to come up sides ½ inch. When boiling, add trimmed asparagus and cook until stalks turn bright green. Remove asparagus from boiling water, put into cold water for a few seconds, and remove from cold water and drain.

Tips, Please

If the asparagus stalks are thicker than ¼-inch, peel the bottoms with a vegetable peeler before cooking. They'll have the tenderness of younger and thinner spears.

3. Spread outside faces of bread with ¾ teaspoon olive oil each. Sprinkle top inside face with vinegar and red pepper flakes (if using).

4. Assemble sandwich with asparagus spears and sun-dried tomatoes. Grill sandwich 5 minutes or until outside faces are golden brown. Serve.

Grilled Portobello Panino

For a filling vegetarian sandwich, you can't go wrong with portobello mushrooms. Here they're paired with roasted bell pepper and scallions.

2 portobello mushrooms with 2-inch diameter caps

2 TB. extra-virgin olive oil

½ Roasted Bell Pepper (recipe in Chapter 5)

2 scallions

1 (4-in.) square Focaccia (recipe in Chapter 3)

1½ tsp. olive oil

Yield: 1 panino
Prep time:
30 minutes
Cook time:
15 minutes
Serving size:
1 panino

1. Heat the grill.

2. Trim stems off mushrooms and save for another use. Cut caps into ½-inch-wide strips. Toss mushrooms in 1½ tablespoons extra-virgin olive oil and cook on grill 5 minutes or until softened. Remove mushrooms from grill and reserve.

3. Slice red pepper into 3 strips and set aside.

4. Split scallions down the middle and trim to fit bread. Toss in remaining ½ tablespoon extra-virgin olive oil and grill 5 minutes or until both sides until barely charred. Set aside.

5. Split Focaccia, and spread outside faces with ¾ teaspoon olive oil each.

6. Assemble sandwich with mushrooms, red pepper strips, and scallions. Grill sandwich 5 minutes or until outside faces are crisp. Serve.

Tips, Please

If you can't find any portobello mushrooms, look for criminis, which are actually young portobellos. Because they're smaller in size, you'll need a few more to cover the bread's surface.

Roasted Root Panino

If asparagus is good in spring, roasted root vegetables are suited to fall and winter days. Here, carrots, parsnip, onion, and arugula combine with blue cheese dressing.

1 carrot

1 parsnip

¼ small onion

1 TB. extra-virgin olive oil

½ cup arugula

1 TB. blue cheese salad dressing

2 slices Sourdough Bread (recipe in Chapter 4)

1½ tsp. olive oil

Yield: 1 panino
Prep time:
45 minutes
Cook time:
20 minutes
Serving size:
1 panino

1. Preheat the oven to 450°F. Heat the grill.

2. Cut carrot in half and split the thicker part in half down the middle.

3. Peel parsnip and cut into ¼-inch slices.

4. Cut onion into ¼-inch slices.

5. Toss carrot, parsnip, and onion in extra-virgin olive oil and add to a roasting pan over high heat. Cook 15 minutes, turning after 7 minutes, or until tender and some edges are slightly charred.

6. Toss arugula with salad dressing.

Secret Ingredient

Roasting the vegetables partly caramelizes their natural sugars and sweetens the taste of the finished panino.

7. Spread outside faces of bread with ¾ teaspoon olive oil each.

8. Assemble vegetables on 1 piece of bread, and top with dressed arugula. Grill sandwich 5 minutes or until outside faces are crisp. Serve.

Artichoke and Cauliflower Salad Panino

With the marinated artichoke hearts and cauliflower paired with spinach and Parmesan cheese, this panino is like having a pickled salad between slices of bread.

2 pepperoncini (optional)

¼ cup prepared marinated artichoke hearts

¼ cup prepared marinated cauliflower

2 slices Sourdough Rye Bread (recipe in Chapter 4)

1½ tsp. olive oil

1 TB. grated Parmesan cheese

½ cup baby leaf spinach

Yield: 1 panino
Prep time: 5 minutes
Cook time: 5 minutes
Serving size: 1 panino

1. Heat the grill.

2. Split pepperoncini (if using) and remove stems and seeds.

3. Cut artichoke hearts into flat pieces.

4. Cut cauliflower into flat pieces.

5. Spread outside faces of bread with ¾ teaspoon olive oil each and coat with cheese.

6. Assemble artichoke hearts and cauliflower on 1 piece of bread. Cover with spinach and top with pepperoncini. Grill sandwich 5 minutes or until cheese coatings crisp. Serve.

Tips, Please

Use a nonstick grill to get the cheese-encrusted faces to release. Otherwise, you'll have a mess on your hands ... and your grill.

Broccoli Panino

Even the pickiest eaters will gobble up this broccoli and cheese delight.

½ cup broccoli florets

2 slices Sourdough Rye Bread (recipe in Chapter 4)

1½ tsp. olive oil

3 slices cheddar cheese

Yield: 1 panino
Prep time: 15 minutes
Cook time: 8 minutes
Serving size: 1 panino

1. Heat the grill.

2. Blanch broccoli in saucepan of boiling water over high heat until bright green. Remove broccoli from boiling water, plunge into cold water to stop the cooking, remove from cold water, and drain.

3. Spread outside faces of bread with ¾ teaspoon olive oil each.

4. Assemble broccoli and cheese on 1 piece of bread. Grill sandwich 5 minutes or until bread is golden brown and cheese melts. Serve.

Tips, Please

To be thrifty, you can take broccoli stalks, peel the outer skin, and slice them to blanch and use in sandwiches as well. Or leftover cooked broccoli lets you skip step 2 altogether.

Chapter 12

International Crusts

In This Chapter

- ◆ Turn appetizers into panini fillings
- ◆ Get your required number of fruit servings in your panino
- ◆ Take a culinary world tour
- ◆ Add new possibilities to your panini with marinated meats and vegetables

No matter what the legend of the Earl of Sandwich, the idea of putting a filling between slices of bread isn't any more the property of the English than of the Italians. It's likely that people have put food between slices of bread for a long time and in many places.

The recipes in this chapter celebrate some of the diversity of cuisine in this world. Relatively few of the dishes will be "official" recipes of other countries. Instead, as in the global pizza recipes in Chapter 8, I concentrated on combinations of flavors that you might find in other parts of the world. Let this be a starting point for your culinary travels.

Panino *Francaise*

Combining bread, pâté, cornichons, and cheese is something you might easily find in France, even if not in the form of a sandwich.

2 slices Ciabatta (recipe in Chapter 4)

1½ tsp. olive oil

¼ lb. pâté, cut into ⅛-inch slices

1 oz. Brie, sliced into 3 pieces

4 cornichons, split down the middle

Yield: 1 panino
Prep time:
15 minutes
Cook time:
5 minutes
Serving size:
1 panino

1. Heat the grill.

2. Split bread, and spread outside faces of bread with ¾ teaspoon olive oil each.

3. Assemble sandwich with pâté, cheese, and cornichons. Grill sandwich 5 minutes or until outside faces are golden brown and cheese is melted. Serve.

Doughfinition

Pâté is a savory loaf that contains meats, poultry, or seafood; spices; and often a lot of fat, served cold spread or sliced on crusty bread or crackers. It is often used as a first course in a formal meal or as an appetizer.

Panino *Italiano*

Slices of prosciutto on cantaloupe is a refreshing Italian appetizer.

1 wedge cantaloupe

2 slices Ciabatta (recipe in Chapter 4)

1½ tsp. olive oil

4 slices prosciutto

Yield: 1 panino
Prep time:
15 minutes
Cook time:
5 minutes
Serving size:
1 panino

1. Heat the grill.

2. Remove rind from melon and cut into 4 slices.

3. Spread outside faces of bread with ¾ teaspoon olive oil each.

4. Assemble sandwich with melon and prosciutto on top. Grill sandwich 5 minutes or until outside faces are golden brown. Serve.

Variation: Not a fan of cantaloupe? You can substitute other types of melon, like honeydew.

Secret Ingredient

To tell if the melon is ripe, smell it. If there's little aroma, find another.

Caribbean Panino

Granted, orange marmalade isn't a Caribbean food, but matching seafood with citrus and cilantro is Caribbean cuisine indeed.

3 jumbo uncooked shrimp

3½ tsp. olive oil

2 slices Whole-Wheat Bread (recipe in Chapter 4)

1 TB. orange marmalade

2 tsp. chopped fresh cilantro

Yield: 1 panino

Prep time:
15 minutes

Cook time:
10 minutes

Serving size:
1 panino

1. Heat the grill.

2. Brush shrimp with 2 teaspoons olive oil, and grill 5 minutes or until cooked through. Cool, remove shell and legs, and devein.

Tips, Please _____

Deveining shrimp involves of shelling the shrimp, using a knife to cut into the back of the shrimp from one end to the other, and removing the black vein.

3. Spread outside faces of bread with ¾ teaspoon olive oil each. Spread inside top with marmalade.

4. Assemble sandwich with shrimp and cilantro on top. Grill sandwich 5 minutes or until outside faces are golden brown. Serve.

Korean Panino

Be sure to have a glass of milk or water handy, because this is one spicy sandwich!

¼ lb. cooked beef tenderloin

1 (4-in.) square Focaccia (recipe in Chapter 3)

1½ tsp. olive oil

1 TB. *kim chee*

Yield: 1 panino
Prep time: 15 minutes
Cook time: 5 minutes
Serving size: 1 panino

1. Heat the grill.

2. Cut beef into ¼-inch slices.

3. Spread outside faces of bread with ¾ teaspoon olive oil each.

4. Assemble sandwich with beef and kim chee. Grill sandwich 5 minutes or until outside faces are golden brown.

Variation: Try this panino with London broil instead of beef tenderloin if you like.

Doughfinition

Kim chee is a Korean pickled cabbage dish. There are many types of kim chee, most of them spicy—that is, when they aren't *very* spicy.

Cuban Panino

Although the ham is also pork, the two variations of the same meat give an interesting contrast.

2 slices Ciabatta (recipe in Chapter 4)

1 TB. butter

2 tsp. prepared mustard

⅛ lb. sliced ham

⅛ lb. sliced pork roast

3 slices Swiss cheese

½ dill pickle, sliced

Yield: 1 panino
Prep time: 15 minutes
Cook time: 5 minutes
Serving size: 1 panino

1. Heat the grill.

2. Split bread and spread butter on outside. Spread mustard on inside top of bread.

3. Assemble sandwich with ham, pork roast, cheese, and pickle slices. Grill sandwich 5 minutes or until outside of bread is golden and cheese melts. Serve.

Variation: Turkey works well in place of the pork roast here.

Secret Ingredient

Next time you find yourself in Miami, look for one of these sandwiches, prevalent in many small restaurants.

Japanese Panino

The pickled ginger adds a tangy pungent note.

¼ lb. boneless skinless chicken

1 TB. teriyaki sauce

2 slices White Bread (recipe in Chapter 4)

1½ tsp. olive oil

1 tsp. wasabi paste (optional)

1 TB. pickled ginger

Yield: 1 panino
Prep time:
2 hours
Cook time:
15 minutes
Serving size:
1 panino

1. Put chicken in a shallow dish, pour teriyaki sauce over, and turn chicken to coat. Let set in refrigerator for 90 minutes.

2. Heat the grill. Grill chicken 10 minutes or until cooked through.

3. Spread outside faces of bread with ¾ teaspoon olive oil each. Spread wasabi (if using) on inside top of bread.

4. Assemble sandwich with chicken and pickled ginger. Grill sandwich 5 minutes or until outside of bread is golden. Serve.

Variation: You can also make the chicken ahead of time or use leftovers.

Tips, Please

You can find wasabi and pickled ginger in Asian markets. If the wasabi comes as a powder, mix 1 teaspoon with enough water to make a paste.

English Panino

This sandwich uses some foundations of English cuisine.

2 slices White Bread (recipe in Chapter 4)

2 tsp. butter

1 TB. Beef Gravy (recipe in Chapter 5)

¼ lb. sliced cooked roast beef

3 slices *Stilton* or cheddar cheese

2 slices red onion

Yield: 1 panino
Prep time:
15 minutes
Cook time:
5 minutes
Serving size:
1 panino

1. Heat the grill.

2. Spread outside faces of bread with 1 teaspoon butter each. Spread inside top side with gravy.

3. Assemble sandwich with roast beef, cheese, and onion. Grill sandwich 5 minutes or until bread is crisp and cheese melted. Serve.

Doughfinition

Stilton is a famous English blue-veined cheese, delicious with toasted nuts and renowned for its pairing with Port wine.

Chapter 13

Morning Mashes

In This Chapter

- ◆ Move beyond the standard McSandwich
- ◆ Transform ordinary breakfast foods into something delicious
- ◆ Turn hot cereal into a panino
- ◆ Pancakes and French toast as sandwich bread? But of course

I understand how breakfast sandwiches have become so popular in restaurants. Combining convenience with good taste is a pretty unbeatable combination. But much of what you see is a combination of a basic theme: eggs and cheese usually accompanied by sausage or bacon.

Not that I'm above an egg sandwich; I can remember enjoying scrambled egg sandwiches even as a child, and I include one variation in this chapter. However, there can be far more to a breakfast sandwich than that. Look at some of the recipes here for some ideas that are out of the ordinary.

Southern Breakfast Panino

Grits and sausage and gravy are both southern favorites. This panino combines the two.

2 breakfast sausage links

¼ cup water

⅛ tsp. ground black pepper

1 TB. White Sauce (recipe in Chapter 5)

2 slices White Bread (recipe in Chapter 4)

2 tsp. butter

¼ cup cooked *grits*

Yield: 1 panino
Prep time: 20 minutes
Cook time: 15 minutes
Serving size: 1 panino

1. Heat the grill.

2. Add sausage links to a small frying pan with water. Bring to boil over high heat and then reduce the heat to medium. Cook 5 minutes or until water evaporates, and continue cooking until sausages are browned.

3. Add ground pepper to White Sauce.

Doughfinition

Grits are coarsely ground grains, usually corn, cooked as a breakfast food in the South.

4. Spread outside faces of bread with 1 teaspoon butter each.

5. Assemble sandwich with grits, sausages, and sauce. Grill sandwich 5 minutes or until outside faces are golden brown. Serve.

Peach French Toast Panino

Because the syrup is on the inside, this is one order of French toast you can eat with your hands.

1 peach

1 egg

2 tsp. milk

1 tsp. sugar

4 slices White Bread (recipe in Chapter 4)

1 TB. maple syrup or honey

Yield: 2 panini

Prep time:
15 minutes

Cook time:
7 minutes

Serving size:
1 panino

1. Heat the grill.

2. Quarter peach and separate pieces, discarding pit. Slice each quarter into thin slices.

3. Lightly beat egg, milk, and sugar in a small bowl. Pour mixture into a wide, shallow container.

4. Dip one side of each slice of bread in egg mixture, letting it soak for 10 seconds; these will be the outsides of the sandwich. Place slices wet side down onto a work surface.

5. For each sandwich, coat dry side of one of the bread slices with ½ tablespoon maple syrup and layer ½ of peach slices on the other. Place maple syrup side on top of peach slices. Grill sandwich 7 minutes or until outside is crisp. Serve.

Secret Ingredient

The reason this recipe, unlike the others, is for 2 panini is because it's hard to find half an egg for the batter, and why waste? Or you can use frozen prepared French toast slices thawed.

Bacon and Egg Panino

A classic breakfast sandwich redone as a panino.

2 slices bacon

4 tsp. butter

1 egg

1 English muffin

1 slice Monterey Jack cheese

Yield: 1 panino
Prep time: 15 minutes
Cook time: 20 minutes
Serving size: 1 panino

1. Heat the grill.

2. Cook bacon in a frying pan over medium heat for 10 minutes or until crispy. Drain and reserve bacon.

3. Clean the pan, and heat again over high heat. Add 2 teaspoons butter. When melted, add egg and fry until white is opaque and firm and the edge is lightly browned. Then turn egg over and cook for 1 minute.

Secret Ingredient

Who needs one of those fast-food breakfast sandwiches? Skip the line at the drive-thru, and whip up your own at home in minutes.

4. Split English muffin. Spread outside faces with 1 teaspoon butter each.

5. Assemble sandwich with egg, bacon, and cheese. Grill sandwich 5 minutes or until outside faces are golden brown and cheese is melted. Serve.

Oatmeal Panino

This breakfast panino is a traditional combination of oatmeal with fruit, brown sugar, and cinnamon.

1 apple

2 slices Sweet Oatmeal Bread (variation in Chapter 4)

2 tsp. butter

1 TB. raisins

1 tsp. brown sugar

¼ tsp. cinnamon

Yield: 1 panino
Prep time:
15 minutes
Cook time:
5 minutes
Serving size:
1 panino

1. Preheat the grill.

2. Peel apple, core, and cut into ⅛-inch slices.

3. Spread outside faces of bread with 1 teaspoon butter each.

4. Assemble apple slices on 1 piece of bread. Sprinkle with raisins, brown sugar, and cinnamon. Grill sandwich 5 minutes or until outside faces are golden brown. Serve.

Tips, Please

Some types of apples—such as the Granny Smiths, Jonathan, and Winesap—are good for cooking, while many others—such as Gala and Red Delicious—are meant for eating raw. If you like the taste of a given apple, it doesn't matter what the "official" use is; include it anyway.

Western Panino

Think of this as a western omelet—complete with onion, bell pepper, ham, and cheese—inside a panino.

4 tsp. butter

1 TB. diced onion

1 TB. diced green bell pepper

1 TB. diced cooked ham

1 egg

1 teaspoon water

2 slices Sourdough Rye Bread (recipe in Chapter 4)

1 slice *Muenster cheese*

Yield: 1 panino
Prep time:
20 minutes
Cook time:
15 minutes
Serving size:
1 panino

1. Heat the grill.

2. Heat a frying pan over medium heat. Add 2 teaspoons butter and melt. Add onion and green bell pepper, and cook until onion is translucent. Add ham and cook 2 minutes or until warmed through.

3. In a small bowl, beat egg with water. Add to the frying pan and scramble.

4. Spread outside faces of bread with 1 teaspoon butter each.

5. Fold egg mixture in ½ and place on one slice of bread. Top with cheese. Grill sandwich 5 minutes or until outside faces are golden brown and cheese melts. Serve.

Doughfinition

Muenster cheese is a German semi-soft cheese.

Short Stack Panino

Pancakes as bread? Why not? This pancake panino, paired with egg, bacon, and maple syrup, will quickly become a breakfast favorite.

3½ tsp. butter

1 egg

2 pieces bacon

2 pancakes (made ahead or frozen)

1½ tsp. maple syrup or honey

Yield: 1 panino
Prep time:
10 minutes
Cook time:
15 minutes
Serving size:
1 panino

1. Heat the grill.

2. Heat a medium frying pan over medium heat. Add bacon to the pan and cook for 10 minutes or until crispy. Drain and reserve bacon.

3. Heat a small frying pan over medium heat. Add 2 teaspoons butter. When butter is melted, add egg and fry for 3 minutes or until cooked through and white is set. Remove egg from pan and set aside.

4. Spread outside faces of pancake with ¾ teaspoon butter each.

5. Put egg topped with bacon on one pancake. Top with maple syrup. Grill sandwich 5 minutes or until outside faces are crisp. Serve.

Secret Ingredient

In my part of Massachusetts, a short stack is 2 pancakes, while a full stack is 3. The next time you're making pancakes, cook a few extra, let them cool, wrap them up, and put them in the freezer. That way you can take out a couple to make a panino.

Fruit Cup Panino

The sugar and butter crust contrast well with the plain yogurt.

1 small wedge cantaloupe

¼ grapefruit

½ orange

½ banana

2 slices Oatmeal Bread (recipe in Chapter 4)

2 tsp. butter

2 tsp. sugar

2 TB. plain yogurt

Yield: 1 panino
Prep time:
30 minutes
Serving size:
1 panino

1. Heat the grill.

2. Cut the rind off cantaloupe and cut into several wedges.

3. Peel grapefruit and divide into sections.

4. Peel orange and divide into sections.

5. Slice banana into ⅛-inch rounds.

6. Spread outside faces of bread with 1 teaspoon butter and 1 teaspoon sugar each.

7. Spread inside of 1 slice of bread with yogurt and arrange fruit on the slice. Grill sandwich 5 minutes or until outside faces are golden brown. Serve.

Tips, Please

Here's another great excuse to break out of the cold-cereal-and-milk breakfast rut. This can also be used for a nice dessert panino.

Glossary

all-purpose flour   Wheat flour that contains only the inner part of the grain with a moderate amount of gluten, making it usable for anything from cakes to gravies.

andouille sausage   A sausage made with highly seasoned pork chitterlings and tripe, and a standard component of many Cajun dishes.

artichoke hearts   The center part of the artichoke flower, often found canned in grocery stores.

arugula   A spicy-peppery garden plant with leaves that resemble a dandelion and have a distinctive—and very sharp—flavor.

bake   To cook in a dry oven. Dry-heat cooking often results in a crisping of the exterior of the food being cooked. Moist-heat cooking, through methods such as steaming, poaching, etc., brings a much different, moist quality to the food.

balsamic vinegar   Vinegar produced primarily in Italy from a specific type of grape and aged in wood barrels. It is heavier, darker, and sweeter than most vinegars.

barbecue   To quick-cook over high heat, or to cook something long and slow in a rich liquid (barbecue sauce).

basil   A flavorful, almost sweet, resinous herb delicious with tomatoes and used in all kinds of Italian- or Mediterranean-style dishes.

biga   *See* levain.

black pepper   A biting and pungent seasoning, freshly ground pepper is a must for many dishes and adds an extra level of flavor and taste.

blanch   To place a food in boiling water for about 1 minute (or less) to partially cook the exterior and then submerge in or rinse with cool water to halt the cooking.

blend   To completely mix something, usually with a blender or food processor, more slowly than beating.

blue cheese   A blue-veined cheese that crumbles easily and has a somewhat soft texture, usually sold in a block. The color is from a flavorful, edible mold that is often added or injected into the cheese.

boil   To heat a liquid to a point where water is forced to turn into steam, causing the liquid to bubble. To boil something is to insert it into boiling water. A rapid boil is when a lot of bubbles form on the surface of the liquid.

Brie   A creamy cow's milk cheese from France with a soft, edible rind and a mild flavor.

broil   To cook in a dry oven under the overhead high-heat element.

brown   To cook in a skillet, turning, until the food's surface is seared and brown in color, to lock in the juices.

bulgur   A wheat kernel that's been steamed, dried, and crushed and is sold in fine and coarse textures.

cake flour   A high-starch, soft, and fine flour used primarily for cakes.

capers   Flavorful buds of a Mediterranean plant, ranging in size from is *nonpareil* (about the size of a small pea) to larger, grape-size caper berries produced in Spain.

caramelize   To cook sugar over low heat until it develops a sweet caramel flavor. The term is increasingly gaining use to describe cooking vegetables (especially onions) or meat in butter or oil over low heat until they soften, sweeten, and develop a caramel color.

caraway   A distinctive spicy seed used for bread, pork, cheese, and cabbage dishes. It is known to reduce stomach upset, which is why it's often paired with, for example, sauerkraut.

cardamom An intense, sweet-smelling spice, common to Indian cooking, used in baking and coffee.

cayenne A fiery spice made from (hot) chili peppers, especially the cayenne chili, a slender, red, and very hot pepper.

cheddar The ubiquitous hard, cow's milk cheese with a rich, buttery flavor that ranges from mellow to sharp. Originally produced in England, cheddar is now produced worldwide.

chevre French for "goat milk cheese," chevre is a typically creamy-salty soft cheese delicious by itself or paired with fruits or chutney. Chevres vary in style from mild and creamy to aged, firm, and flavorful.

chiles (or **chilies**) Any one of many different "hot" peppers, ranging in intensity from the relatively mild ancho pepper to the blisteringly hot habañero.

chives A member of the onion family, chives grow in bunches of long leaves that resemble tall grass or the green tops of onions and offer a light onion flavor.

chop To cut into pieces, usually qualified by an adverb such as "*coarsely* chopped," or by a size measurement such as "chopped into ½-inch pieces." "Finely chopped" is much closer to mince.

chorizo A spiced pork sausage eaten alone and as a component in many recipes.

chutney A thick condiment often served with Indian curries made with fruits and/or vegetables with vinegar, sugar, and spices.

ciabatta A type of rustic bread found in Italy.

cilantro A member of the parsley family and used in Mexican cooking (especially salsa) and some Asian dishes. Use in moderation, as the flavor can overwhelm. The seed of the cilantro is the spice coriander.

cinnamon A sweet, rich, aromatic spice commonly used in baking or desserts. Cinnamon can also be used for delicious and interesting entrées.

clarified butter   Butter heated until the solids separate out, any water evaporates, and you can pour off the clear liquid that won't smoke when heated.

cornichon   A small sweet-and-sour pickle. It's the French version of a gherkin, though typically smaller than the U.S. variety.

crimini mushrooms   A relative of the white button mushroom but brown in color and with a richer flavor. The larger, fully grown version is the portobello. *See also* portobello mushrooms.

curry   Rich, spicy, Indian-style sauces and the dishes prepared with them. A curry uses curry powder as its base seasoning.

curry powder   A ground blend of rich and flavorful spices used as a basis for curry and many other Indian-influenced dishes. Common ingredients include hot pepper, nutmeg, cumin, cinnamon, pepper, and turmeric. Some curry can also be found in paste form.

devein   The removal of the dark vein from the back of shrimp with a sharp knife.

dice   To cut into small cubes about ¼-inch square.

dill   A herb perfect for eggs, salmon, cheese dishes, and, of course, vegetables (pickles!).

dough scraper   A metal or plastic rectangular blade that lets you scrape dough off a work surface.

dried yeast   Baking yeast that comes in packets and jars and needs dissolving in warm water to come back to life.

drizzle   To lightly sprinkle drops of a liquid over food, often as the finishing touch to a dish.

extra-virgin olive oil   *See* olive oil.

fennel   In seed form, a fragrant, licorice-tasting herb. The bulbs have a much milder flavor and a celerylike crunch and are used as a vegetable in salads or cooked recipes.

feta A white, crumbly, sharp, and salty cheese popular in Greek cooking and on salads. Traditional feta is usually made with sheep milk, but feta-style cheese can be made from sheep, cow, or goat milk.

fillet A piece of meat or seafood with the bones removed.

flake To break into thin sections, as with fish.

flaeskeaeggekage A Danish version of quiche, but with a more custardlike consistency.

flatbread A type of bread that is formed in a flat shape before baking, as though someone took an iron to it.

floret The flower or bud end of broccoli or cauliflower.

flour Ground-up grains. Wheat is the most familiar for bread dough, and that's more or less what you need for pizza or panini. You could also mix in other types, such as oats, rye, buckwheat, or rice. *See also* all-purpose flour; bread flour; cake flour; whole-wheat flour.

fold To combine a dense and light mixture with a circular action from the middle of the bowl.

food processor A kitchen appliance made of a bowl or container with changeable blades at the bottom that can mix, cut, and knead.

fry *See* sauté.

garbanzo beans (or **chickpeas**) A yellow-gold, roundish bean used as the base ingredient in hummus. They are high in fiber and low in fat.

garlic A member of the onion family, a pungent and flavorful element in many savory dishes. A garlic bulb contains multiple cloves. Each clove, when chopped, provides about 1 teaspoon garlic. Most recipes call for cloves or chopped garlic by the teaspoon.

ginger Available in fresh root or dried, ground form, ginger adds a pungent, sweet, and spicy quality to a dish.

gluten The protein in wheat flours that is the natural elastic band that gives bread its stretch and texture.

gouda   A mild Dutch cheese made from cow's milk.

grate   To shave into tiny pieces using a sharp rasp or grater.

grind   To reduce a large, hard substance, often a seasoning such as peppercorns, to the consistency of sand.

grits   Coarsely ground grains, usually corn, cooked as a breakfast food in the South.

Gruyère   A rich, sharp cow's milk cheese made in Switzerland that has a nutty flavor.

Havarti   A creamy, Danish, mild cow's milk cheese perhaps most enjoyed in its herbed versions such as Havarti with dill.

horseradish   A sharp, spicy root that forms the flavor base in many condiments from cocktail sauce to sharp mustards. Prepared horseradish contains vinegar and oil, among other ingredients. Use pure horseradish much more sparingly than the prepared version, or try cutting it with sour cream.

hummus   A thick, Middle Eastern spread made of puréed garbanzo beans, lemon juice, olive oil, garlic, and often tahini (sesame seed paste).

kalamata olives   Traditionally from Greece, these medium-small long black olives have a smoky rich flavor.

kim chee   A Korean pickled cabbage dish. There are many types of kim chee, most of them spicy—that is, when they aren't *very* spicy.

knead   To work dough to make it pliable so it holds gas bubbles as it bakes. Kneading is fundamental in the process of making yeast breads.

knockwurst   A mild German sausage resembling a fat hot dog.

kosher salt   A coarse-grained salt made without any additives or iodine. It can have a subtler flavor and doesn't dissolve as fast when sprinkled on food.

levain Also called, in various languages, a poolish, biga, and sponge, to name a few, it is a mixture that effectively lets the dough rise an extra time and also improves the texture.

live yeast A form of yeast for baking that comes in cubes or blocks.

loaf pan A rectangular form that keeps a loaf of bread in a regular symmetrical shape, like sandwich types you'd find in a grocery store.

Manchego A Spanish cheese that can be either semi-soft or hard and made of either cow or sheep milk.

mascarpone A thick, creamy, spreadable cheese, traditionally from Italy.

mince To cut into very small pieces smaller than diced pieces, about 1/8 inch or smaller.

Monterey Jack A mild cheese.

mozzarella di bufala Campana The original type of mozzarella, made of the milk of water buffalos. It's more delicate in texture and flavor than mozzarella made from cow's milk.

Muenster A German semi-soft cheese.

nutmeg A sweet, fragrant, musky spice used primarily in baking.

olive oil A fragrant liquid produced by crushing or pressing olives. Extra-virgin olive oil—the most flavorful and highest quality—is produced from the first pressing of a batch of olives; oil is also produced from later pressings.

olives The fruit of the olive tree commonly grown on all sides of the Mediterranean. Black olives are also called ripe olives. Green olives are immature, although they are also widely eaten. *See also* kalamata olives.

oyster mushrooms Medium off-white mushrooms with a delicate flavor.

panino (plural: *panini*) A grilled sandwich, an Italian sandwich whether grilled or not, or any roll in Italy.

Parmesan   A hard, dry, flavorful cheese primarily used grated or shredded as a seasoning for Italian-style dishes.

Parmigiano Reggiano   Real Italian Parmesan cheese.

pâté   A savory loaf that contains meats, poultry, or seafood; spices; and often a lot of fat, served cold spread or sliced on crusty bread or crackers.

peel   A handle with a flat blade at one end that helps get breads and pizzas in and out of the oven.

pepper jelly   A type of prepared jelly, found in many grocery stores and specialty food shops, incorporating peppers. It may be a sweet pepper or hot type.

pesto   A thick spread or sauce made with fresh basil leaves, garlic, olive oil, pine nuts, and Parmesan cheese. Some newer versions are made with other herbs.

pimiento   A Spanish-style pepper usually sold roasted, skinned, and pickled.

pine nuts (also **pignoli** or **piñon**)   Nuts grown on pine trees, that are rich (read: high fat), flavorful, and a bit pine-y. Pine nuts are a traditional component of pesto and add a wonderful hearty crunch to many other recipes.

pissaladiere   A French-style pizza that comes from Provence has anchovies. It's a great snack or light meal.

pita bread   A flat, hollow wheat bread often used for sandwiches or sliced, pizza style, into slices. Terrific soft with dips or baked or broiled as a vehicle for other ingredients.

pizza stone   Preheated with the oven, a pizza stone cooks a crust to a delicious, crispy, pizza-parlor texture. It also holds heat well, so a pizza or other food removed from the oven on the stone stay hot for as long as $1/2$ hour at the table.

pizzaiolo (plural: *pizzaioli*)   An Italian pizza maker.

poolish   *See* levain.

porcini mushrooms   Rich and flavorful mushrooms used in rice and Italian-style dishes.

portobello mushrooms   A mature and larger form of the smaller crimini mushroom, portobellos are brownish, chewy, and flavorful. Often served as whole caps, grilled, and as thin sautéed slices. *See also* crimini mushrooms.

preheat   To turn on an oven, broiler, or other cooking appliance in advance of cooking so the temperature will be at the desired level when the assembled dish is ready for cooking.

prosciutto   Dry, salt-cured ham, that originated in Italy.

purée   To reduce a food to a thick, creamy texture, usually using a blender or food processor.

reduce   To boil or simmer a broth or sauce to remove some of the water content, resulting in more concentrated flavor and color.

reserve   To hold a specified ingredient for another use later in the recipe.

rice vinegar   Vinegar produced from fermented rice or rice wine, popular in Asian-style dishes. Different from rice wine vinegar.

ricotta   A fresh Italian cheese smoother than cottage cheese with a slightly sweet flavor.

roast   To cook something uncovered in an oven, usually without additional liquid.

rosemary   A pungent, sweet herb used with chicken, pork, fish, and especially lamb. A little of it goes a long way.

salsa   A style of mixing fresh vegetables and/or fresh fruit in a coarse chop. Salsa can be spicy or not, fruit-based or not, and served as a starter on its own (with chips, for example) or as a companion to a main course.

sauté   To pan-cook over lower heat than used for frying.

savory   A popular herb with a fresh, woody taste.

sear   To quickly brown the exterior of a food, especially meat, over high heat to preserve interior moisture.

sea salt   This type of salt comes in flakes that is harvested from ocean water and has a more complex flavor—and more expensive price tag.

semolina   A type of flour made of durum wheat often used in pasta.

shallot   A member of the onion family that grows in a bulb somewhat like garlic and has a milder onion flavor. When a recipe calls for shallot, use the entire bulb.

shiitake mushrooms   Large, dark brown mushrooms with a hearty, meaty flavor. Can be used either fresh or dried, grilled or as a component in other recipes and as a flavoring source for broth.

shred   To cut into many long, thin slices.

simmer   To boil gently so the liquid barely bubbles.

skillet (also **frying pan**)   A generally heavy, flat-bottomed metal pan with a handle designed to cook food over heat on a stovetop or campfire.

slice   To cut into thin pieces.

sponge   *See* levain.

stand mixer   Machinery for mixing, whipping, and kneading. It sits on top of a counter or table and a powerful motor moves the unit's blade through whatever needs the workout.

Stilton   The famous English blue-veined cheese, delicious with toasted nuts and renowned for its pairing with Port wine.

tabbouleh   A Middle Eastern salad with chopped tomatoes, parsley, mint, and bulgar wheat.

table salt   The ordinary kind you put into the shaker and can buy at the grocery store.

tahini   A paste made from sesame seeds used to flavor many Middle Eastern recipes.

teriyaki   A Japanese-style sauce composed of soy sauce, rice wine, ginger, and sugar that works well with seafood as well as most meats.

tipo 00 flour   An Italian flour that's finely ground and good for pizza dough.

toast   To heat something, usually bread, so it's browned and crisp.

tofu   A cheeselike substance made from soybeans and soy milk.

vinegar   An acidic liquid widely used as dressing and seasoning, often made from fermented grapes, apples, or rice. *See also* balsamic vinegar; cider vinegar; rice vinegar; white vinegar; wine vinegar.

walnuts   A rich, slightly woody flavored nut.

wasabi   Japanese horseradish, a fiery, pungent condiment used with many Japanese-style dishes. Most often sold as a powder; add water to create a paste.

whisk   To rapidly mix, introducing air to the mixture.

white mushrooms   Button mushrooms. When fresh, they have an earthy smell and an appealing "soft crunch."

whole-wheat flour   Wheat flour that contains the entire grain.

wine vinegar   Vinegar produced from red or white wine.

wok   A pan for quick-cooking.

Worcestershire sauce   Originally developed in India and containing tamarind, this spicy sauce is used as a seasoning for many meats and other dishes.

yeast   A type of tiny organism that chews up starch and burps out carbon dioxide making the bubbles that cause dough to rise.

zest   Small slivers of peel, usually from a citrus fruit such as lemon, lime, or orange.

Index

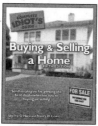

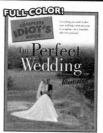

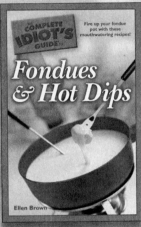